T0209457

An Analysis of

John Berger's

Ways of Seeing

Katja Lang
with
Emmanouil Kalkanis

Published by Macat International Ltd
24:13 Coda Centre, 189 Munster Road, London SW6 6AW.

Distributed exclusively by Routledge
2 Park Square, Milton Park, Abingdon, Oxon OX14 4RN
711 Third Avenue, New York, NY 10017, USA

Routledge is an imprint of the Taylor & Francis Group, an informa business

www.macat.com
info@macat.com

Cataloguing in Publication Data
A catalogue record for this book is available from the British Library.
Library of Congress Cataloguing-in-Publication Data is available upon request.
Cover illustration:David Newton

ISBN 978-1-912303-93-9 (hardback)
ISBN 978-1-912284-64-1 (paperback)
ISBN 978-1-912284-78-8 (e-book)

CONTENTS

THE MACAT LIBRARY

The Macat Library is a series of unique academic explorations of seminal works in the humanities and social sciences – books and papers that have had a significant and widely recognised impact on their disciplines. It has been created to serve as much more than just a summary of what lies between the covers of a great book. It illuminates and explores the influences on, ideas of, and impact of that book. Our goal is to offer a learning resource that encourages critical thinking and fosters a better, deeper understanding of important ideas.

Each publication is divided into three Sections: Influences, Ideas, and Impact. Each Section has four Modules. These explore every important facet of the work, and the responses to it.

This Section-Module structure makes a Macat Library book easy to use, but it has another important feature. Because each Macat book is written to the same format, it is possible (and encouraged!) to cross-reference multiple Macat books along the same lines of inquiry or research. This allows the reader to open up interesting interdisciplinary pathways.

To further aid your reading, lists of glossary terms and people mentioned are included at the end of this book (these are indicated by an asterisk [*] throughout) – as well as a list of works cited.

Macat has worked with the University of Cambridge to identify the elements of critical thinking and understand the ways in which six different skills combine to enable effective thinking.
Three allow us to fully understand a problem; three more give us the tools to solve it. Together, these six skills make up the **PACIER** model of critical thinking. They are:

ANALYSIS – understanding how an argument is built
EVALUATION – exploring the strengths and weaknesses of an argument
INTERPRETATION – understanding issues of meaning

CREATIVE THINKING – coming up with new ideas and fresh connections
PROBLEM-SOLVING – producing strong solutions
REASONING – creating strong arguments

To find out more, visit **WWW.MACAT.COM.**

CRITICAL THINKING AND *WAYS OF SEEING*

Primary critical thinking skill: ANALYSIS
Secondary critical thinking skill: CREATIVE THINKING

John Berger's 1972 book *Ways of Seeing* comprises seven essays (three of which are purely pictorial) about visual arts and the way we understand paintings. The book pushed boundaries, accusing academics and connoisseurs of "mystifying" art and making it accessible only to an elite minority instead of the general public. Berger's view was that artworks could be made accessible to everyone, educated or not, by exploring the language of art and the social context within which an artwork was created.

To make his case, Berger created and constructed new contexts for understanding and interacting with works of art. His work gains much of its impact from the strength and coherence of his arguments, a product of his exceptional ability to set out a persuasive case in which each part of the argument has a precise, delineated function. Berger's arguments are detailed and complete. He deals with counter-arguments and counter-claims, draws clear distinctions between arguments and explanations, and arranges his case in an effective sequence.

Using direct observation of masterworks, combined with his analysis of contemporary visual culture and critical exploration of works of fine art that have been considered significant, Berger's work can also be seen as a delicate exercise in the critical thinking skill of creative thinking. Indeed, understanding Berger's methods of analysis means you might never look at visual arts—particularly paintings—in the same way again.

ABOUT THE AUTHOR OF THE ORIGINAL WORK

Born in 1926, **John Berger** was one of the most influential art critics of his generation. Best known for his 1972 BBC television series *Ways of Seeing*, he was enormously prolific throughout his life, but his print companion to the four half-hour programs is still regarded one of the best introductions to visual culture and how to think critically about art.

As a lifelong Marxist and a vehement critic of capitalism, Berger attacked the elite art establishment and its class bias. He died in 2017 at the age of 90.

ABOUT THE AUTHORS OF THE ANALYSIS

Katja Lang holds a Master's degree in the history of collecting and collections from Glasgow and an MEd in Research Practice from the University of Cambridge.

Emmanouil Kalkanis was awarded his PhD by the University of Durham and holds an MA in Museum Studies from Reinwardt Academy, Amsterdam. His research focuses on the early-modern reception of classical antiquity, particularly vases, and employs both archeological and art-historical approaches. Dr Kalkanis currently working for the Greek Ministry of Culture and is involved in an excavation project in western Greece.

ABOUT MACAT

GREAT WORKS FOR CRITICAL THINKING

Macat is focused on making the ideas of the world's great thinkers accessible and comprehensible to everybody, everywhere, in ways that promote the development of enhanced critical thinking skills.

It works with leading academics from the world's top universities to produce new analyses that focus on the ideas and the impact of the most influential works ever written across a wide variety of academic disciplines. Each of the works that sit at the heart of its growing library is an enduring example of great thinking. But by setting them in context – and looking at the influences that shaped their authors, as well as the responses they provoked – Macat encourages readers to look at these classics and game-changers with fresh eyes. Readers learn to think, engage and challenge their ideas, rather than simply accepting them.

'Macat offers an amazing first-of-its-kind tool for interdisciplinary learning and research. Its focus on works that transformed their disciplines and its rigorous approach, drawing on the world's leading experts and educational institutions, opens up a world-class education to anyone.'

Andreas Schleicher
Director for Education and Skills, Organisation for Economic Co-operation and Development

'Macat is taking on some of the major challenges in university education … They have drawn together a strong team of active academics who are producing teaching materials that are novel in the breadth of their approach.'

Prof Lord Broers,
former Vice-Chancellor of the University of Cambridge

'The Macat vision is exceptionally exciting. It focuses upon new modes of learning which analyse and explain seminal texts which have profoundly influenced world thinking and so social and economic development. It promotes the kind of critical thinking which is essential for any society and economy. This is the learning of the future.'

Rt Hon Charles Clarke, former UK Secretary of State for Education

'The Macat analyses provide immediate access to the critical conversation surrounding the books that have shaped their respective discipline, which will make them an invaluable resource to all of those, students and teachers, working in the field.'

Professor William Tronzo, University of California at San Diego

WAYS IN TO THE TEXT

KEY POINTS

- John Berger was among the most important and influential British art critics and writers of the twentieth century.

- *Ways of Seeing* argues that the interpretation of art was often based on certain assumptions made by art critics.

- *Ways of Seeing* is a landmark text for presenting a materialist* analysis of European art to a mass audience in an accessible form.

Who Was John Berger?

John Berger (1926–2017), was a British art critic, novelist, painter, poet, and scriptwriter best known for his essays on art criticism, his sociological* writings, his Marxist* views, and his controversial opinions on modern art.* Starting in the early 1950s, he wrote art criticism for the *New Statesman*, a left-wing periodical. He became notorious in the mid-1950s for supporting the Kitchen Sink* movement and calling for a new type of social realism* in art. In the mid-1960s, he presented two films directed by Michael Gill, one about the French painter Fernand Léger* and the other on the self-taught French outsider artist and postman, Ferdinand Cheval.* The study of Cheval demonstrated Berger's willingness to look beyond the canon of great artists. Berger was also one of the first art critics to comment on the objectification* of women in art and the extent to which they are often depicted in a particular way in order to be admired by male spectators. This approach encouraged his readers to look at art in a new light and to question long-established assumptions about culture in a wider context.

In the 1970s, Berger was already a respected art critic. He had written on a wide range of topics and in a variety of media, "fluidly moving between fiction and essay, art criticism and memoir, Berger has emerged as a sort of 'Zen Master' of the written word,"[1] as one critic observed. Related to Marxist ideas, his goal was not to offer answers as such, but to challenge the reader's assumptions in order to start a process of questioning, thus opening up and democratizing interpretation. Berger's work as a critic and art historian pioneered ideas in favor of an existential view of the artist and the artwork. In his pioneering effort, for example, toward a revaluation and critical assessment of Picasso's* art, Berger claimed that as Picasso's paintings themselves became commodities, the artist drained his artistic creativity from all possibilities and ran out of subjects for his paintings.[2]

What Does *Ways of Seeing* Say?

Ways of Seeing was written in 1972 and was based on ideas contained in a BBC television series of the same name. The series comprised four thirty-minute episodes exploring different themes in the visual arts. It was well received and seen to represent a turning point in the history and analysis of art. Following the success of the series, Berger and his team were asked to translate its ideas into a book. The resulting work is a collection of seven essays, three of which are purely pictorial, consisting only of pictures of artworks and largely without text.

Ways of Seeing was written in England at a time when fine art (particularly European painting) was seen as a commodity belonging to the wealthy and the educated. Berger's central aim was the demystification of art, which had been "mystified" by the "cultural establishment." Only elite academics belonged to this establishment, and in Berger's opinion they made artworks unnecessarily remote from the ordinary person, thus keeping art as the preserve of the rich and educated.

In *Ways of Seeing* Berger sets out to show how paintings can be understood and interpreted through their socio-historical context— the place and time within which they were created and with reference to the life of the author or artist. Using specific pictorial examples by such famous artists as Dutch Golden Age* painter Frans Hals* or German Renaissance* artist Hans Holbein the Younger,* Berger suggests that what we see is always influenced by a multitude of assumptions we hold about such things as beauty, form, class, taste, and gender. Berger asks the reader to consider and even confront these assumptions, and take them into account when interpreting works of art. Another of Berger's argument is that aesthetics* based on the consideration of "beautifully made objects" are of no value because ways of looking at art have been utterly changed by the development of mechanical means of producing and reproducing images.

Berger addressed such issues by writing in a style that was coherent and easy to follow. The process of inquiry on the part of the reader is integral to *Ways of Seeing*, highlighted on the last page of the book, which states: "To be continued by the reader." To summarize, John Berger's *Ways of Seeing* revolutionized the way in which art is read and understood, and although it was written in 1972, many of the ideas expressed are still current. It was exceptional in the amount of discussion it provoked. Although the author's influence may have waxed and waned over time, the fact that *Ways of Seeing* is still in print is a testimony to its continued relevance, particularly with reference to visual culture and advertising. After four decades, the book has sold more than a million copies.[3]

Why Does *Ways of Seeing* Matter?

The uniqueness of Berger's approach in *Ways of Seeing* is that he sets out to start what he refers to as a process of questioning, aiming to provoke a reaction in people and thus open up new debates. The author argues that you do not need to be a connoisseur or an academic to appreciate a work of art. He urges the public to study images carefully without making assumptions.

Both the socio-economic climate and the work of rival schools of thought should be taken into account when considering John Berger's *Ways of Seeing*; the latter not least because they show by comparison how revolutionary Berger's ideas were at the time, going against convention, and how modern his way of thinking was. It is difficult to discern which interpretation of art is "correct," as the schools of thought focus on different angles and argue from opposing standpoints, but Berger's work presents a fresh and accessible way to look at fine art, which the general public, and not just a well-educated elite, can understand.

As a classic attack on traditional art-historical thinking and an influence on the emergent field of cultural studies, *Ways of Seeing* has been a very popular advocate of that same tradition making art history relevant to a wide audience. Berger's arguments are applicable to many issues that society deals with today. Themes like the politics of gender* and the portrayal of the female nude, the illusion of free choice (such as the manipulative nature of advertising images), and the power of the image in terms of its effect on consumerism,* continue to dominate contemporary debates.

The importance of *Ways of Seeing* extends beyond academic study, posing questions about the kind of images that we constantly encounter on a daily basis within a modern context. To some degree this is even more the case today as we are exposed to advertising, and virtual and digital images more than ever before. As such, certain themes in the book remain sharply relevant and can be more clearly understood in the context of Internet and social media culture. Arguably they are even more applicable in today's dramatically different world of rapid viral circulation of images than they were in the 1970s.

NOTES

1   Anderson Tepper, "At Work: John Berger on *Bento's Sketchbook*," *The Paris Review* (November 22, 2011), accessed June 11, 2017, https://www.theparisreview.org/blog/2011/11/22/john-berger-on-%E2%80%98bento%E2%80%99s-sketchbook%E2%80%99/.

2   John Berger, *Success and Failure of Picasso* (London: Penguin Books, 1965).

3   "John Berger, the Author of Ways of Seeing, has died aged 90," Obituary, *The Art Newspaper* (January 3, 2017), accessed July 23, 2017, http://theartnewspaper.com/news/obituary/john-berger-the-author-of-ways-of-seeing-has-died-aged-90.

THE AUTHOR AND THE HISTORICAL CONTEXT

KEY POINTS

- *Ways of Seeing* was a groundbreaking and controversial work of art criticism and visual culture when it was published in England in 1972.
- Berger's professional life was deeply shaped by a series of talks on art for the BBC and his writings on art criticism for the *New Statesman*.
- The "mystification" of art and Berger's Marxist ideas shaped the ways he responded to the visual culture of his era.

Why Read This Text?

In *Ways of Seeing* (1972), John Berger highlights the importance of how seeing may be affected by a variety of factors, and as such there is no *one* true way of seeing something. As a collection of essays that can be read in any order, the book begins by stating:"Seeing comes before words. The child looks and recognizes before it can speak."[1] Berger argues that the relationship between what we see and what we know is never settled, as what we see is always affected and shaped by our knowledge or beliefs. Everyone might look at the same thing, but each person perceives it differently.

The book was revolutionary: it made a great impact when it was published in the early 1970s—a period dominated by traditional views of what art was and how it should be interpreted. According to Berger, at this time paintings were subject to a process he calls "mystification,"[2] through which critics talked about art in a way that excluded people from a non-academic background. A review article from 1979 sums

> **❝** When I was eighteen I went into the army where ...
> I was expected to become an officer—which I refused
> to do. Because of this I remained in a recruiting unit
> ... and this was actually the first time that I lived with
> working class men. This had a great effect on me, not
> directly politically but socially. **❞**
>
> John Berger interview, *Marxism Today*

this up: "Berger uses the analysis of the painting of Frans Hals ... by a prominent art historian to illustrate the way in which the cultural 'expert' goes about setting up barriers between the work of art and the ordinary viewer, all in the name of a 'correct and subtle' interpretation."[3] *Ways of Seeing*, instead proposed a new, direct way of experiencing the visual arts, based on a detailed analysis of the image itself and its context—both of its making and its consumption. Almost 50 years have passed since its original publication, but *Ways of Seeing* remains crisp, young, and relevant, and a reference point in discussing visual culture.

Author's Life

John Berger, was born in London, England in 1926 to Stanley J. D. Berger, a minor public official, and Miriam Branson, a working-class woman from Bermondsey, south London. He was raised "in only moderate comfort, with little high culture,* in what he described as a working-class home."[4] Despite this he was privately educated at a boarding school in Oxford before gaining a scholarship to study at the Central School of Art in London at the age of 16. Between 1944 and 1946 he served in the British Army and was posted to a Belfast training depot. After the army, he went to Chelsea School of Art under the tutelage of Henry Moore,* another formative experience: in "painting, drawing, writing, and talking to Henry Moore ... life was suddenly so full," he confessed in 2005. "Until 1954, I'd only ever thought of being a painter, but I earned my money when and where I could. You could say I drifted into writing."[5]

Berger subsequently spent his time between teaching drawing part-time at St Mary's teacher training college in Strawberry Hill, southwest London, and exhibiting his work at the Leicester, Redfern, and Wildenstein galleries. However, it wasn't until the early 1950s when he began giving a series of talks on art for the BBC World Service that he found his feet. He started writing art criticism for the *New Statesman* in 1951, beginning a 10-year period as its controversial, but highly influential art critic, often singling out for praise an artist nobody else had heard of. There, he made a name for himself by antagonizing nearly everyone in the art world "in prose that was beautifully spare and precise but heavily moralizing and also frequently humorless … he took on giants like Jackson Pollock,* whom he criticized as talented failure for being unable to 'see or think beyond the decadence of the culture to which he belongs.'"[6]

In the mid-1970s, when his critical influence was at his height in Britain, he moved to Paris, and then to Geneva. He later decided to move to a remote peasant community, Quincy, nestled in the French Alps. There, he lived for more than 40 years with his American wife, Beverly Bancroft, who died in 2013, and their son, Yves.

Author's Background

As noted by the English writer Geoff Dyer,* *Ways of Seeing*, like many of Berger's other works, deals with two themes that dominated Berger's life and as a result had an influence on his work: the mystery of art and the lived experience of the oppressed. In a book of his selected essays, Berger expresses his hatred for bourgeois culture and society as reflected in the field of art. He talks of the great injustice and hypocrisy that surrounds this field.[7] This radical view could perhaps be linked to his experiences during the early 1950s, as in his interviews Berger often refers to his memories of the Cold War.* Oppression was endemic during this time and Berger felt that he had to speak up about this injustice, turning to the medium of writing as a result. "It seemed that one really had to protest in order to make this terminal catastrophe even slightly less likely," Berger says.[8]

From 1952 to 1962, Berger worked as an art critic for the *New Statesman*, a left-wing periodical writing in favor of social realism and exploring Marxist ideas. It is important to note how opposed these views were to the privileged background of private education and art school Berger had come from. His outspokenness meant he often fought to have his work published as he had intended it: "Consequently every week after I had written my article I had to fight for it line by line, adjective by adjective, against constant editorial cavilling.*"[9] Berger's experience during this period of rigid conformism shaped *Ways of Seeing*, in which he aims to speak the truth and offer an alternative view of the art world, one that is open to everyone, irrespective of social class.

NOTES

1   John Berger, *Ways of Seeing* (London: Penguin, 2008), 7.

2   Berger, *Ways of Seeing,* 11.

3   Peter Steven, "*The Ways of Seeing* – Against Kenneth Clark, for John Berger," *Jump Cut: A Review of Contemporary Media 20* (May 1979), 7-8.

4   Randy Kennedy, "John Berger, Provocative Art Critic, Dies at 90," *The New York Times*, (January 02, 2017), accessed June 19, 2017, https:/www.nytimes.com/2017/01/02/arts/design/john-berger-provocative-art-critic-dies-at-90.html?_r=0.

5   Quoted in Sean O'Hagan, "A Radical Returns," *The Guardian*, (April 03, 2005), accessed June 19, 2017, https:/www.theguardian.com/artanddesign/2005/apr/03/art.art1.

6   Kennedy, "John Berger, Provocative Art Critic, Dies at 90."

7   Geoff Dyer and John Berger, *John Berger/Selected Essays*, ed. Geoff Dyer (London: Bloomsbury, 2001), 4.

8   Quoted in Andrew Lambirth, "Arts: John Berger: Ways of Seeing, Ways of Biking," *The Independent*, Saturday (January 17, 1998), accessed July 01, 2017, http://www.independent.co.uk/life-style/arts-john-berger-ways-of-seeing-ways-of-biking-1139132.html.

9   Dyer and Berger, *John Berger/Selected Essays*, 4.

MODULE 2
ACADEMIC CONTEXT

KEY POINTS

- With *Ways of Seeing*, Berger wrote about visual culture in a period that saw a range of radical ideas being implemented in the arts.

- *Ways of Seeing* challenges the idea that artworks are the preserve of the rich, accessible to an elite minority.

- The intellectual stimulus for *Ways of Seeing* was Walter Benjamin's* 1936 essay "The Work of Art in the Age of Mechanical Reproduction."

The Work In Its Context

In 1971 John Berger was commissioned by the BBC to make a television series on topics of his choosing. Following its success, BBC Publications commissioned Berger and the program's director, Mike Dibb,* to turn the television series into a book. Together with graphic designer Richard Hollis, script consultant Chris Fox, and artist Sven Blomberg, Berger published *Ways of Seeing* in 1972. The ideas were largely adapted from the four-part television series, and the book and the series shared the same title. It is important to remember this publication history when considering the work's context.

The relationship between television and the visual arts at that time was, as one scholar observes, "a clash between culture at its most popular and accessible and culture at its most exclusive and elitist.*"[1] When Berger entered the scene a decade or so earlier the contemporary disciplinary boundaries that characterize the field of visual culture today had little currency. It was Berger's successful attempt to make connections across social arenas—such as art history,

> ❝ There has been a determined effort on the part of some British intellectuals to use television to popularize high culture. Kenneth Clark, for instance, employed the medium to propagate and preserve the values of European high culture, while John Berger used the medium to demystify that very same culture and, indeed, television itself. ❞
>
> John A. Walker, Arts TV: A History of Arts Television in Britain

cultural analysis, and communication theory—that marks the most radical nature of his intervention. Although there was neither a single, dominant style nor a logical sequence of movements in art being produced at the time, much new British art of the 1970s did have a distinctive character influenced by left-wing politicization. "It was during this decade that artists attempted to implement a range of radical ideas conceived in the 1960s [such as] conceptual art,* feminist art,* ecological art* ... performance art* and video art,* indeed all forms of art with a sense of social purpose ... These kinds of art did not appeal to the existing artworld [because] they challenged and sought alternatives to the gallery system based on the sale of art objects/commodities to the wealthy."[2]

However, the preoccupation of the period in which Berger wrote *Ways of Seeing* was with authoritative analysis of the work of key artists, such as paintings by the Old Masters.* Berger's work ran counter to that dominant ideology. The book appeared just three years after the famous art historian Kenneth Clark created his influential television series *Civilisation*, which upheld traditional methods of interpretation. Berger refers to this process as "mystification;" a process that puts up barriers between the work of art and the ordinary viewer. The traditional interpretation of art required more than mere observation; you needed an academic knowledge in order to understand and fully appreciate a work of art, unlocked through deciphering esoteric clues. However, Berger strongly opposes this approach, arguing that looking closely at an image reveals a lot of information, even to an ordinary viewer who is not an expert.

Overview Of The Field

The question of interpretation is significant as the language of art had already been explored by other art critics, including Seymour Slive,* Lawrence Gowing,* and Kenneth Clark, all of whose work Berger refers to in *Ways of Seeing.* Berger often disagrees with their methods of describing art, accusing them of mystifying art objects. He offers an alternative view, asking the readers themselves to look at paintings carefully and consider the time and place within which they were created. The standard model of studying, appreciating, and looking at art in the late 1960s and early 1970s can be summarized by Kenneth Clark's *Civilisation*, broadcast in 1969. Through the thirteen-part series, Clark judged and expounded on how civilization is defined by a succession of God-gifted geniuses, who produced masterpieces that he found "tasteful" and "eternal." Moreover, the series only covered western Europe, and all the Great Masters featured were white men.

Berger rejected this patrician approach to art and his *Ways of Seeing* is often regarded as a response to Clark's *Civilisation* (1969), although it was not meant to be seen as such.[3] Berger went against the notion of art belonging to the wealthy and highly educated. Berger also sheds light on how women are portrayed in art (and in advertising), his feminist assertions challenging traditional views about paintings by the Old Masters. While, for example, Clark wrote about the skill with which nudes were executed,[4] Berger focuses on the social context of their creation.

Academic Influences

The origins of Berger's *Ways of Seeing* can already be discerned in some of his earlier work, where he avoids the traditional categories of art in favor of an existential view of the artist and the artwork. In these, Berger credits the writings of the Hungarian art historian Frederick Antal* for teaching him how to write history and interpret the visual arts in their social, economic, political, and ideological context, and his book on Picasso was dedicated to the art historian Max Raphael.* Antal had a particular influence on Berger; it was his *Florentine Painting and its Social Background* (1948) that showed Berger what a social history of art might look like. "For a time, Berger was his [Antal's] unofficial pupil," John Walker* remarks in his history of arts TV in Britain.[5] Berger was a radical figure, and according to Bob Light, writing an obituary for Berger in the *Socialist Review*, "the problem for radicals like him ..." was that Marxist art criticism was hopelessly corrupted by what Berger called "'pseudo-Marxist mystification' and Stalinist aesthetics; both were little more than a projection of the interests of the Russian ruling class,* indeed often little more than an intellectualisation of Stalin's* own vulgar tastes."[6] So Berger had to re-invent his own language of seeing.

According to Mike Dibb, co-author and director of *Ways of Seeing*, the inspiration for the first essay came at a time when the English translation of Walter Benjamin's essay "The Work of Art in the Age of Mechanical Reproduction" was first published.[7] In making the first episode of the television series, Berger and his team overtly tried to make this text as accessible as possible, with Benjamin credited at the end of this episode. Benjamin's essay looked at the democratizing impact of the availability of images through modern reproduction,[8] and opposed the method of art criticism practiced by academics in the late 1960s. Kenneth Clark, in particular, as Berger argues, "totally represented the connoisseur explaining to the populace 'this is how it is'. *Ways of Seeing* was [instead] a collaboration. We wanted people to ask questions. It was the opposite of the ivory tower."[9] This was the point at which the concept for the television series first crystallized; the book itself should therefore be seen within the same context.

NOTES

1   Martin McLoone, "Presenters, Artists, and Heroes," *Circa*, 31 (November–December 1986), 10–4.

2   John Walker, *Arts TV: A History of Arts Television in Britain*, (London: John Libbey, 1993), 87–8.

3   Peter Fuller, *Seeing Through Berger* (London: The Claridge Press, 1988), 69–74.

4   Kenneth Clark, *The Nude* (London: Penguin, 1960).

5   Walker, *Arts TV*, 91–2.

6   Bob Light, "John Berger Opened Up New Ways of Seeing," *Socialist Review* (February 2017), accessed June 20, 2017, http://socialistreview.org.uk/421/john-berger-opened-new-ways-seeing.

7   Juliette Kristensen, "Making *Ways of Seeing*: A Conversation with Mike Dibb and Richard Hollis," *Journal of Visual Culture* 11:2 (August 2012): 181–95.

8   Walter Benjamin, "The Work of Art in the Age of Mechanical Reproduction," in *Illuminations: Essays and Reflections*, ed. Hannah Adrendt (London: Cape, 1968).

9   Philip Maughan, "'I Think the Dead are With Us': John Berger at 88," *New Statesman*, (June 11, 2015), accessed June 20, 2017, http://www.newstatesman.com/culture/2015/06/i-think-dead-are-us-john-berger-88.

MODULE 3
THE PROBLEM

KEY POINTS

- *Ways of Seeing* is a book about visual culture and how it was being shaped both by traditional scholarship and contemporary mass media.
- Berger's approach to art was in sharp contrast to the insights provided by conventional art historians in respect of the oil painting tradition.
- Berger's approach targeted those not initiated into the language of art criticism and philosophy.

Core Question

Many of the themes John Berger addresses in *Ways of Seeing* are particular to the way we understand and look at paintings. At its core, the book is a personal reaction to the enormous impact of publicity, television, image reproduction, capitalism,* and a discussion of gender and ethnicity. In fact, it was the purpose of the TV series "to demonstrate to a mass audience just how masterworks of the past are in complicity with the economic system."[1]

At the time of publication, much debate in Western art history centered on the connoisseurship* and the interpretation of works accepted as masterpieces (painted by Old Masters). The skill with which such paintings were produced was often highlighted and praised by art critics. Critics did not fully acknowledge or consider the socio-cultural circumstances within which a painting was created. Instead, they talked about art in a way that was not accessible to most people.

> 66 Benjamin's 'The Work of Art in the Age of Mechanical Reproduction' was crucial not only because it directly inspired the content of the first [of Berger's television] program but also because the issue of reproduction's impact upon the traditional fine arts and upon our perception of art, applied to the series as a whole and indeed to all arts broadcasting. 99
>
> John A. Walker, Arts TV: A History of Arts Television in Britain

At the end of the first essay in *Ways of Seeing*, Berger writes: "Many of the ideas in the preceding essay have been taken from another, written over 40 years ago by … Walter Benjamin."[2] Although Benjamin's essay had been written decades earlier, its publication in English translation came only shortly before Berger was commissioned by the BBC to produce the television series *Ways of Seeing*, which directly preceded the book. Thus, some of the content (especially the first essay) in the book is a product of "received ideas," as Benjamin's essay inspired Berger to write critically about art and the ways of looking at it, which Berger openly acknowledges. This does not mean that the ideas presented in the book were not fresh. Indeed, as Mike Dibb recently explained, they were "very new at the moment … in terms of addressing the tradition of European painting in that way … I don't think anything had been done like that before."[3]

The Participants

In a period (late 1960s and early 1970s) that saw the war in Vietnam* still raging, the coming to prominence of peace and civil rights movements* in the United States, the women's liberation movement,* student unrest in France in May 1968,* intense consumerism, and the rise of radical artists and intellectuals, the very idea of culture was changing. *Ways of Seeing* is best positioned not only amid these rapid political and social changes, but also alongside those texts that depart from traditional art historical thinking in favor of delineating how art is represented in the modern age. Walter Benjamin's essay, "The Work of Art in the Age of Mechanical Reproduction" coincides with Berger's arguments because they both explain that artworks have lost their original meaning; with photography and film making, art has come to change the perceptions of the viewer. Like Benjamin, Berger claims that "in the age of pictorial reproduction the meaning of paintings is no longer attached to them; their meaning becomes transmittable ..."[4]

In contrast to Benjamin, however, Berger makes a serious critique of the official institutions that mystify fine art, such as museums, galleries, and especially art history texts. According to Berger, by avoiding a work's represented content and focusing instead on the aesthetics of technique, art history more often obscures the true meaning of an artwork. Thus, Berger goes against the official line in reading the Renaissance Great Masters, and *Ways of Seeing* sparks debate and controversy among leading contemporary scholars. He uses the example of Frans Hals's *Regents of the Old Men's Alms House*, and then quotes the American art historian Seymour Slive to support his argument. From Berger's perspective, one of the Regents appears drunk and disheveled, as the painter's intention was to represent a type of decadence of "the new characters and expressions created by capitalism."[5] For Slive, any mention of drunkenness is a libel. By avoiding any possible political message that the bourgeoisie* were corrupt and, therefore, explaining away what might otherwise be evident, Slive prefers to limit his interpretative analysis strictly to the artist's formal skill and technique. In doing this, the book signals an important turning point in art history scholarship, for it promotes a process of questioning traditional ways of looking at art that centered around connoisseurship and artistic skill.

The Contemporary Debate

Although art and culture have proved difficult subjects for Marxists to tackle—since Marxism is primarily a critique of political economy*— there are many writers, such as Theodor Adorno,* Arnold Hauser,* Ernst Fischer,* and Raymond Williams* who have provided useful insights on these subjects. Some essays in *Ways of Seeing* indeed took inspiration from the work of others: Walter Benjamin's essay "The Work of Art in the Age of Mechanical Reproduction" informs Berger's explanations of how what we see is influenced by a host of assumptions relating to age, gender, beauty, and taste. As Mike Dibb explains: "It was a very shared evolution of an argument, and one of the very first early decisions was to use the Walter Benjamin essay … as a point of departure."[6] Berger diverges, however, from Benjamin significantly in that *Ways of Seeing* is far more conversational and easy to read by those not initiated into the language of art criticism and philosophy.

Other essays in Berger's book were directed as a repudiation of the work of famous art critics: Berger challenges Kenneth Clark and his followers in dealing with the issue of ownership in connection with oil paintings. If Kenneth Clark's "self-congratulatory and patrician televisualization of Ernst Gombrich's* *The Story of Art* had made visible the ideological and sociological function of art history at the time," Griselda Pollock* argues, "Berger, emerging out of what was to us an occluded Marxist and socialist humanist tradition* of British realism* that had been so vivid in British culture during the 1950s and 1960s, arrived on the TV screens and in the bookshop just when we needed a ready-made and persuasive critique of the art establishment, advertising images of women."[7]

NOTES

1   John Adkins Richardson, "Ways Seeing by John Berger," *The Journal of Aesthetic Education*, 8:4 (October 1974), 112.

2   John Berger, *Ways of Seeing* (London: Penguin, 2008), 34.

3   ABC Radio. "Exhibit A: John Berger – Changing the Way We See – Part 4." ABC Radio, Accessed July 15, 2017, http://www.abc.net.au/rn/legacy/programs/sunmorn/stories/s1335486.htm.

4   Berger, *Ways of Seeing*, 24.

5   Berger, *Ways of Seeing*, 14.

6   ABC Radio. "Exhibit A: John Berger ..."

7   Griselda Pollock, "Muscular Defences," *Journal of Visual Culture* 11: 2 (August 2012): 127–31, 127.

MODULE 4
THE AUTHOR'S CONTRIBUTION

KEY POINTS

* In *Ways of Seeing*, John Berger questioned some of the bourgeois ways in which academics looked at art.
* Berger's approach changed the way in which the language of visual culture was talked about.
* Berger combined cultural and political analysis, aesthetic insights, and sharp modernist eyes in a clear, dynamic, and accessible form.

Author's Aims

John Berger never saw art appreciation as an elite activity. In *Ways of Seeing*, he sets out to popularize the most advanced theories of modernity and visual culture that were then current. His historical perspective, reinforced by his Marxist ideas, was combined with a slight distance from modern art and a desire to interpret it in his own way. *Ways of Seeing* was unique in the way that it presented each artwork in its social and historical contexts—and those contexts included now as well as then. For him, the real question is: to whom does the art of the past properly belong? This is not a matter of aesthetics or technique, but a matter of class power. So, what Berger was trying to do was to look back at those images of past works of art, not purely as a code for some political message, "but to remind ourselves of our fundamental freedoms and social purpose—and especially these ideas about desire and the way in which the role of women had been so much elevated in art … and at the same time so denigrated and reduced into this peculiar object of both control and fear."[1] Berger intended to use those images in ways never intended by

> 66 What strikes me as strange in retrospect is the elegance and confidence of *Ways of Seeing* in its accessible formulations, its everyday vocabularies, and ... its telling class politics ... Oil paintings depict things that a class of people want, own and then celebrate as possessions that confirm their power to want and to own. This belongs to a historical moment. 99
>
> Griselda Pollock, "Muscular Defences," *Journal of Visual Culture*

their makers. He therefore warned viewers to be skeptical of his own arrangements of words and pictures.

Approach

John Berger arrived at the key concepts of *Ways of Seeing* through direct observation of masterworks, combining this with his analysis of contemporary visual culture and critical exploration of works of fine art that have been considered significant. Throughout his essays, Berger uses illustrations of key works by Old Masters like Rembrandt* or Rubens* to support the claims he makes, for instance that women are represented as objects in oil paintings. Although *Ways of Seeing* offers insights on a range of topics, it does not, by the author's own admission, pretend to deal with more than certain aspects of each subject.[2] John Berger's intention was to address the accessibility of art, convey his belief that it should be available to everyone, and highlight the fact that at the time this book appeared (in 1972), this was not the case.

Overall, Berger's writing is easily accessible, providing an aid to understanding his intent. Berger uses visual referencing to illustrate his points clearly and coherently, which is why *Ways of Seeing* is often considered an entry-level book on art theory and criticism. His style is more inclusive than that of many of his contemporaries, such as the prominent art historian Kenneth Clark, who wrote predominantly for a highly educated audience. In order for the text to be a continuous argument, the images came exactly at the moment where the reader wants to refer to them. His arguments are not implied, but rather his opinions are expressed openly, even confrontationally, as he seeks to make art accessible to everyone using clear and direct language. The themes exist in stand-alone essays, but sometimes they merge and occasionally the author refers to one essay within another. *Ways of Seeing* was designed to be read in any order, so the reader is not required to approach the essays from the beginning in order to understand Berger's arguments and chain of thought.

Contribution In Context

Berger's writings focus on diverse themes, ranging from artists to thinkers, from photography to painting. His work often provides original insight.[3] However, many of the ideas for *Ways of Seeing* had already been evident in some of his other work, including essays he had written on women in art or his Booker Prize-winning novel, *G.*, which follows a young man on his journey to establish a sexual career in Europe. In his art criticism, as well as his sociological and anthropological studies, Berger's primary concerns were always experience, meaning, and the study of the individual, whether artifact or person. For instance, to understand both the work and the painter, he paid close attention to the individual thing, so we should not think the painter as separated from his own engagement with the form and substance of his work.

The book, indeed, "is in some ways the least original of all his previous writing."[4] His approach to art came directly into the public eye in the four-part BBC television series that preceded his book of the same name, but his style of blending Marxist awareness and sensibility as well as art theory with attention to small details and personal stories developed much earlier, in essays for the *New Statesman* and also in his first novel *A Painter of Our Time*. Published in 1958, the book is a tale about the disappearance of a fictional exiled Hungarian painter living in London in the early 1950s when Hungary is undergoing social and political upheaval. It was one of Berger's most comprehensive reflections on art, sexuality, revolution, capitalism, politics, propaganda, human nature, and society. Throughout that period, "especially in the 50s he [Berger] was enormously influenced by émigré artists living in London … and a number of other Central European Marxist artists who lived in Europe."[5] After all, it was this capacity to decode the visual culture, to show how women have become objectified as passive objects of consumption, or explain that what gets lost is the meaning of the value of things in themselves, that connects Berger not just to Marxism, Walter Benjamin, and others, but also the French philosophers Camus* and Merleau-Ponty.*[6]

Ways of Seeing was hugely influential "for its argument that it is too easy, and lazy, to read every work of art and each experience through a single frame of reference."[7] Referring to the BBC television series that preceded Berger's book, another reviewer remarks that, "Arnold Hauser and Meyer Shapiro have given us [already] similar analyses that were, respectively, of greater intellectual sweep and infinitely more penetrating long before Berger commenced as art critic. But, then, no art historical writing could possibly have had the influence that a few moments of television can provide."[8]

NOTES

1   ABC Radio. "Exhibit A: John Berger – Changing the Way We See – Part 4." ABC Radio, Accessed July 15, 2017. http://www.abc.net.au/rn/legacy/programs/sunmorn/stories/s1335486.htm.

2   John Berger, *Ways of Seeing* (London: Penguin, 2008), 5.

3   Examples can be found in Geoff Dyer and John Berger, *John Berger/Selected Essays*, ed. Geoff Dyer (London: Bloomsbury, 2001).

4   ABC Radio. "Exhibit A: John Berger …"

5   ABC Radio. "Exhibit A: John Berger …"

SECTION 2
IDEAS

MAIN IDEAS

KEY POINTS

- In *Ways of Seeing*, Berger examines critically the difference between looking at art and seeing it.

- The central idea of *Ways of Seeing* is that visual experience was never innocent, even in the most exclusive areas of high art.

- The author asks the reader to consider the arguments made within, and then make up their own mind about what they choose to believe.

Key Themes

Broadly speaking, there are four main themes in *Ways of Seeing*, which John Berger explores in separate essays in this seminal text. The first theme looks at establishing the relationship between what we see and what we know, and how our assumptions—about form, class, beauty, taste, and gender—affect how we see a painting. The second is about the role of women as subjects in artwork, discussing the female nude in particular. Berger shows how women are depicted as objects to please their male-orientated audience, and how their sexual nature is particularly highlighted in the representation of female nude. The third theme deals with European oil painting and the relationship between the subjects depicted and ownership. Berger argues, for example, that people often desire to own what is depicted in a painting. The final theme takes the idea of ownership into modern consumerist society, looking at the power of imagery in advertising, with particular regard to photography. By constructing a link between the tradition of oil painting and images used for advertising, the author shows how

> ❝ But there is also another sense in which seeing comes before words. It is seeing which establishes our place in the surrounding world; we explain that world with words, but words can never undo the fact that we are surrounded by it. The relation between what we see and what we know is never settled. ❞
>
> John Berger, *Ways of Seeing*

powerful such images are: how they can influence the way we feel and even manipulate us.

Exploring The Ideas

In the first essay Berger argues that the art of the past "is being mystified because a privileged minority is striving to invent a history which can retrospectively justify the role of the ruling classes, and such a justification can no longer make sense in modern terms."[1] Despite mainstream art history's obsession with skill, Berger argues, truly quality painting is often overlooked; museums, he says, frequently hang mediocre paintings alongside great ones. Berger contends that the art establishment attributes value on the basis of a painting being an original rather than technical virtuosity. Berger's key argument here rests on the idea that since not just everyone can possess the "real" painting, the ruling class art establishment imbues one-of-a-kind objects with tremendous monetary and therefore cultural value. In this framework, the skill of the artist becomes secondary to the presence of the picture itself.

The female nude in Western painting comes next. According to Berger, she was there to feed an appetite of male sexual desire. She did not have desires of her own; she existed to be looked at, posed in such a way that her body was there only to be consumed. Of course, Berger wrote there was hypocrisy in this, too: "You painted a naked woman because you enjoyed looking at her … put a mirror in her hand and you called the painting 'Vanity'. Thus morally condemning the woman's nakedness you had depicted for your own pleasure."[2] Borrowing Kenneth Clark's distinction between the nude and the naked, the idealized and the actual, Berger argued that the nude has always exemplified the vision of woman as passive possession; his analysis spared only those artists who, like Rembrandt, preferred the naked to the nude, and painted pictures of individual, assertive women.

Berger also wanted to show how concealed ideological contexts exist in high art. In doing this, he riled art scholars by claiming that one purpose of European oil painting was always to confirm its patrons in the pleasure of ownership of their possessions. Berger believes that no other medium could have served the interests of the market economy's ruling class as effectively as oil painting. In contrast to the immovability of the fresco,* fixed as it was in the exclusive geographical locations of cathedrals and palaces, oil paintings were portable objects that could be bought and sold for more affordable prices. The owner of the painting possessed both the picture and whatever was represented within its frame. This helped create a new "way of seeing the world, which was ultimately determined by new attitudes to property and exchange that found its visual expression in the oil painting, and could not have found it in any other visual art form."[3]

Berger is known to be sympathetic to the ideas of Socialist humanism,* and *Ways of Seeing* is sometimes seen as an example of Marxist ideology. Indeed, there are numerous implicit statements that are compatible with leftist thoughts. "Capitalism," he writes, "survives by forcing the majority, whom it exploits, to define their own interest as narrowly as possible."[4] He gives examples of sharply contrasting images published in magazines, advertising for beauty products and editorial images of refugees from Pakistan on the same page. Publicity, Berger argues, "exerts an enormous influence and is a political phenomenon of great importance. It recognized nothing except the power to acquire. All other human faculties or needs are made subsidiary to this power."[5]

Language And Expression

In *Ways of Seeing*, each theme seeks to address the public in a way that is non-elitist, equal and direct, by using language that is understandable to an ordinary reader and by keeping each essay short and supported with visual examples by well-known artists. As a result of this approach, the four essays of the book read like a collection of small independent, but interconnected insights, rather than a coherent whole. The images are inserted into the running text, precisely in the positions where they become self-explanatory, so they are part of the story, and do not break the flow of reading.[6] The text, with its heavily indented paragraphs and sans serif font, was unusual and broke every conventional typographical rule. In an attempt to replicate the experience of the television viewer, the bold type throughout was designed to render the weight of the words as heavy as that of the images. These factors all contribute to *Ways of Seeing* being ideally suited to those who are new to art criticism and art writing in general. It is regarded as a good introduction to this topic. The individual ideas presented do not just exist to present answers, but encourage the reader to engage with the work through a process of questioning.

Berger's approach to socio-historical analysis of artworks makes the style of *Ways of Seeing* highly distinctive as a reading of visual arts with new concepts or terms, such as "mystification" and "cultural establishment." "Mystification is the process of explaining away what otherwise might be evident,"[7] says Berger. In contrast to Seymour Slive's analysis of Frans Hals's last two paintings, Berger thinks that Hals was one of the first artists to depict the social relations, expressions, and characters created by capitalism. Berger asserts that the art historian's language severs the paintings from their historical situation, seeing this high culture approach as preventing contemporary people from "seeing" the art of the past and thus to situate themselves in history. Discussing the special relationship between oil painting and property "that played a certain role even in the development of landscape painting,*"[8] Berger also uses another unique concept. He believes that among the pleasures that the Gainsborough* portrait of Mr and Mrs Andrews gave to the owners was "the pleasure of seeing themselves depicted as landowners." However, he argues, the essential character of the painting has been obscured "by an almost universal misreading of the relationship between its 'tradition' and its 'masters' … This allows the 'cultural establishment' to project for a little longer its false rationalised image of itself."[9]

NOTES

1   John Berger, *Ways of Seeing* (London: Penguin, 2008), 11.

2   Berger, *Ways of Seeing,* 51.

3   Berger, *Ways of Seeing*, 87.

4   Berger, *Ways of Seeing*, 154.

5   Berger, *Ways of Seeing*, 153.

6   See Juliette Kristensen, "Making *Ways of Seeing*: A Conversation with Mike Dibb and Richard Hollis," *Journal of Visual Culture* 11:2 (August 2012), 181–95.

7   Berger, *Ways of Seeing*, 15.

8   Berger, *Ways of Seeing*, 106.

9   Berger, *Ways of Seeing*, 109.

SECONDARY IDEAS

KEY POINTS

- *Ways of Seeing* is direct when it comes to its core argument. It is, therefore, difficult to discern secondary ideas within the text.

- Berger emphasizes the role of the art market* in the way we look and appreciate paintings.

- The range of visual-culture material Berger drew together allows readers to take away their own meaning from the text through the three pictorial essays.

Other Ideas

The core themes in John Berger's *Ways of Seeing* are presented in four different essays (there are also three purely pictorial essays, which echo these themes). These are the importance of social and historical context when looking at art; the demystification of art objects and art criticism as well as the portrayal of women and their role as subjects in artworks; the relation between subject matter and ownership in European oil painting; and the power of present-day advertising imagery. It is hard to pinpoint any other, subordinate themes, as the main thrust of the work is to question traditional ways of looking at art, which were based on connoisseurship and judging artistic skill. However, a few ideas put forward by Berger in *Ways of Seeing* are *not* core to the work, but can still be considered important.

The extent to which the value of an artwork is affirmed, and further defined by the price it fetches on the market, is a theme that was only touched on by the author. Berger's brief discussion of the so-called "genre"* picture—the picture of "low life" and how oil painting

> 66 The National Gallery sells more reproductions of Leonardo's* *The Virgin and Child* ... than any other picture ... It became famous because an American wanted to buy it for two and a half million pounds. Now ... it has acquired a new kind of impressiveness. Not because of what it shows ... [but] because of its market value. 99
>
> John Berger, *Ways of Seeing*

lent plausibility to a sentimental lie—should also be considered as a secondary theme. The frequent reproduction of paintings with words around them and the impact this may have on the viewer's perception is also important here.

Exploring The Ideas

In *Ways of Seeing*, Berger argues that an image's meaning, what it shows, is no longer the thing that strikes the observer as unique. Instead it is the object itself—its value that defines it, and its value depends upon its rarity. This value is affirmed and gauged by the price it fetches on the market. Berger points out that this "bogus religiosity which now surrounds original works of art, and which is ultimately dependent upon their market value, has become the substitute for what paintings lost when the camera made them reproducible."[1]

In the fifth essay Berger argues that the analogy between possessing and the way of seeing that is incorporated in oil painting, is a factor usually ignored by art experts and historians. To support his argument, he goes further to explore genre painting. According to him, "genre" pictures were particularly popular with the newly arrived bourgeoisie, who identified themselves not with the characters painted, but with the moral that the scene illustrated. There is a lie here though: "namely that it was the honest and hard-working who prospered, and that the good-for-nothings deservedly had nothing."[2] He then uses the example of Adriaen Brouwer* who was the "only exceptional 'genre' painter."[3] Although his pictures were painted with a bitter and direct realism, nobody ever bought them. By contrast other "genre" paintings—like those by a "master" such as Hals, depicted poor people smiling "as they offer what they have for sale." Such pictures assert two things, Berger concludes: "that the poor are happy, and that the better-off are a source of hope for the world."[4]

Among other things, Berger also uses pictorial examples to demonstrate how our assumptions, and the context surrounding a work, affects our judgment or understanding of it. He uses a well-known Van Gogh* painting to demonstrate this point. He shows us two versions of one painting, the first of which is not annotated, but when the reader turns the page he finds the same picture accompanied by a handwritten note that reads: "This is the last picture that Van Gogh painted before he killed himself." "This simple but powerful exercise illustrates Berger's point of the impact words can have on an image."[5]

Overlooked

If anything has been neglected in *Ways of Seeing*, it is perhaps in the three essays that contain only images of artworks, with only infrequent captions detailing the name of the artist or the title of the work. According to John Walker, these were inserted between chapters in order to "compensate for the lack of moving images."[6] After all, the adaptation from a television series into a written text was not without its challenges. According to Berger himself, as he explains in a "Note to the Reader" at the beginning of the book, "These purely pictorial essays are intended to raise as many questions as the verbal essays … sometimes no information at all is given about the images reproduced because it seemed to us that such information might distract from the points being made."[7] These may even deserve reconsideration, as they have assumed greater relevance in today's society. The low cost of color printing has increased the number of images that we encounter in our daily lives. In particular, the essay showing how women are viewed as objects, drawing on examples from oil painting to modern-day photography, illustrates an interesting journey through time; the issue of gender politics continues to dominate contemporary discussion.

At the same time, there seemed to be "an effort to avoid making the text *too* radical. Striking to us today, at both the visual and textual level, is the almost total omission of any critical analysis of race discourse in *Ways of Seeing.*"[8] There are only some minor references to "non-European traditions" and to works depicting colonial power and slavery. The first instance is when a comparison is made between the supine nude in European painting and women in "Indian art, Persian art, African art, and Pre-Columbian art" where "nakedness is never supine in this way."[9] It is not as if Berger lets us forget that racial and ethnic bias drive the structure and content of images in oil painting and mass culture, it is more that he carefully avoids mentioning it directly. Commentary regarding cultural difference is reserved for a close reading of newspapers and magazines that pair, for example, an advertisement of British wealth on the same page as the image of poverty in Pakistan, but it remains a class analysis for Berger.[10] It has been argued that although race politics in England hit a fever pitch right at the time *Ways of Seeing* was published and broadcast (e.g. due to restrictive immigration policies put in place in the 1960s and 1970s, it was easier for Old (white) Commonwealth* citizens to obtain residency in Britain than New (black) Commonwealth citizens), "understating matters of racial difference was perhaps the most effective and least alienating gesture that could have been made at the time to a majority white audience."[11]

NOTES

1 John Berger, *Ways of Seeing* (London: Penguin), 23.

2 Berger, *Ways of Seeing*, 103.

3 Berger, *Ways of Seeing*, 103.

4 Berger, *Ways of Seeing*, 104.

5 Peter Bil'ak, "*Ways of Seeing* – Book Review," *Back Cover*, no. 1 (2008), accessed July 14, 2017, http://www.typotheque.com/articles/ways_of_seeing_book_review.

6 John Walker, *Arts TV: A History of Arts Television in Britain* (London: John Libbey, 1993), 10.

7 Berger, *Ways of Seeing*, "Note to the Reader."

8 Jennifer A. Gonzalez, "Calculated Oversight? Resisting Race in *Ways of Seeing*," *Journal of Visual Culture* 11:2 (August 2012), 137–40.

9 Berger, *Ways of Seeing*, 53.

10 Berger, *Ways of Seeing*, 152.

11 Gonzalez, "Calculated Oversight?" 139.

ACHIEVEMENT

KEY POINTS

- *Ways of Seeing* achieved its goal of breathing new life into art historical debates and making it easier for the wider audience to study visual culture.
- Berger's controversial ideas shaped the field of social art history.*
- Although Berger's ideas have been very influential, they are not without limitations.

Assessing The Argument

John Berger's *Ways of Seeing* has had a great impact. First published in England in 1972 by the BBC and Penguin, it is now under the latter's Modern Classics imprint, which denotes its landmark status. It was effective in reaching its target audience when it was first published, but it continues to offer insight on how art can be understood, with references to fine art, film, photography and media studies. *Ways of Seeing* sparked debate and controversy not only among prominent art critics, but also among the general public. Berger's Marxist point of view has also paved the way for art historians such as T. J. Clark,* who has taken the field of art history in a direction that is not preoccupied with traditional ways of looking at art.

Over the past 40 years John Berger's *Ways of Seeing* has been influential outside of its initial field of art criticism, as its ideas have been dissected and informed new ways of thinking. One could argue that Berger has achieved his main objective, which was to start a process of questioning. He has accomplished this by bringing new ideas to our consciousness, such as the objectification of women in art,

> ❝ *Ways of Seeing* was significant in several respects.
> It was the first to present a materialist analysis of
> European art to a mass audience in an accessible form,
> the first to reflect the influence of an emerging women's
> movement of the late 1960s/early 1970s ... and the first
> to incorporate a decoding of advertising imagery. ❞
> John A. Walker, Arts TV: A History of Arts Television in Britain

which in turn gave birth to a new set of theories and ideas, informing our understanding of new subjects, such as that of feminism*. For Berger, as one reviewer has put it, "the success of his book might not be measured so much by the answers we produce to his questions but instead in the silence we inhabit to formulate the answer."[1]

Achievement In Context

Berger's contribution to the development of art criticism and critical art history was to be pioneering. *Ways of Seeing* became a key work in cultural studies, art history, and visual studies, and its ideas have had a tremendous influence on art history since the 1970s. The book's aim was to speak to a wide audience by addressing its readership in a non-elite manner. By doing so, it points out a link between social background and an interest in the arts. Through the use of a table,[2] Berger illustrates how a person with a privileged upbringing is more likely to be interested in the subject, while someone from a less privileged background is less likely to be exposed to it.

Berger believed mightily in the power of painting, but *Ways of Seeing* was, above all, an attempt to demystify the subject. Being openly indebted to the Marxist philosopher Walter Benjamin's reverberant essay "The Work of Art in the Age of Mechanical Reproduction," Berger thought that "the preachiness and preciousness around fine art was used, ideologically, to whitewash the past that produced it. In key ways, *Ways of Seeing* is about the democratic potential of mass media in making the classics accessible to the average person, by allowing images to slip free of the stilted atmosphere of the museum, and be reintegrated into life."[3]

Some of the core themes presented in *Ways of Seeing* are bound to a particular time and place. The period in which the book was first written was a crucial factor in who it was written for and in how it was perceived by its audience. As Richard Howells explains in his publication *Visual Culture*, the political atmosphere in institutes of higher education in Britain, Europe and America in the 1960s and 1970s was more radical than it is today.[4] As such, John Berger's art-theoretical attack on capitalism was very current and of its time, as it spoke to a specific audience. Even the whole idea of the male gaze* "… pretty obvious to us now, but at the time, certainly on television, not many people had thought about the European nude in that way … the way Berger says that the painters and spectator owners were usually men and the persons treated as objects were usually women."[5] *Ways of Seeing* director, Mike Dibb, also remarks: "the time it was made, in the early 1970s … the women's movement was really developing … and therefore it was a good moment to be making that kind of analysis."[6]

Limitations

Ways of Seeing unveiled something that had always been there but remained under the veil of traditional scholarship and art criticism. It showed this potential plurality and activity for all to see, realize, and act upon. The way people look at art has never been the same since. This enhanced its impact outside academia. At the same time, the depth of his insights made it also an enduring reference for critical art history and, in a sense, contributed to generating the visual studies movement. In *Ways of Seeing* Berger focuses his criticisms on Western art and the tradition of European painting. Berger's system of analysis carries its own limitations though. From time to time he makes references to other cultures, only to illustrate his points more clearly in a direct comparison between them. In the essays in which he talks about female nudity and women's submissive depictions, he explains that his argument does not apply to the art of non–European traditions, such as Indian, Persian, African, or Pre–Columbian art.[7]

One other important aspect is that before the publication of *Ways of Seeing*, most of Berger's ideas had already been included in the BBC television series of the same name aired in 1972. The process of adapting a work to a different medium does not often succeed in taking the parameters of the new medium fully into account. However, the adaptation of *Ways of Seeing* from TV to a book format is unusual in that it maintains the extraordinary clarity of Berger's key arguments. In doing so, Berger and his team successfully make use of the limitations and conventions of print publishing. On the TV screen, for instance, Berger uses silence as an active agent of change in how we see things. In the book, the simple act of turning a page serves much the same purpose in comparing two views of a Van Gogh painting with different annotations.

NOTES

1   Pratibha Rai, "Review: *Ways of Seeing*," *The Oxford Culture Review* (April 04, 2017), accessed July 03, 2017, https://theoxfordculturereview.com/2017/04/04/review-ways-of-seeing/.

2   John Berger, *Ways of Seeing* (London: Penguin, 2008), 24.

3   Ben Davis, "The Unfinished Business of John Berger," *Artnet* (January 6, 2017), accessed June 24, 2017, https://news.artnet.com/art-world/the-unfinished-business-of-john-berger-806741.

4   Richard Howells and Joaquim Negreiros, *Visual Culture*, 2nd ed. (Cambridge: Polity Press, 2012), 96.

5   ABC Radio. "Exhibit A: John Berger – Changing the Way We See – Part 4." ABC Radio, Accessed July 15, 2017. http://www.abc.net.au/rn/legacy/programs/sunmorn/stories/s1335486.htm.

6   ABC Radio. "Exhibit A: John Berger ..."

7   Berger, *Ways of Seeing*, 55.

MODULE 8
PLACE IN THE AUTHOR'S WORK

KEY POINTS

- *Ways of Seeing* was not Berger's first book, but it was the one that brought him fame, and got widespread attention in the press.

- John Berger never ceased being productive; *Ways of Seeing* was neither the start of Berger's lifelong focus on visual arts and culture nor the end.

- The themes contained in Berger's *Ways of Seeing* have inspired and attracted many writers and thinkers in various academic fields.

Positioning

John Berger was one of the most influential British intellectuals of the past 50 years. He was best known for his seminal book of art criticism, *Ways of Seeing*, which was published in 1972 and has shaped the thinking of at least two generations of artists and students. As far back as the late 1950s, however, he had dealt with exile and displacement in his first novel, *A Painter of Our Time*, which has since become one of the defining socio-political issues of our time. His writing ranges across forms and his subject matter varies from Picasso to world poverty, from photography to the plight of landless peasantry.

It was in 1972, though, that he came into his own in spectacular fashion. The controversial success of *Ways of Seeing* was followed by his sole excursion into post-modernist* fiction with *G.,* a novel that won him the fledging Booker Prize. As one reviewer remarked, "Long before the stage-managed hysteria that now surrounds the Booker,

> **❝** Through the steadiness of his convictions, through the humanity that filled everything he wrote, through the force of his examples as someone who was at ease with being non-conformist, he made the questions of art seem worth grappling with as part of grappling with the questions of the world we live in. That is beyond reproach. **❞**
>
> Ben Davis, *Artnet News*

Berger created a storm of controversy by using his acceptance speech to castigate Booker McConnel* for their historical trading interests in the West Indies,*"[1] then he announced that he was donating half his prize money to the Black Panthers.*

Integration

One of the biggest obstacles in writing about Berger's work as a whole is the wide range of texts he produced in his lifetime. However, despite a long and prolific career, Berger is most famous for his 1972 book and BBC TV series *Ways of Seeing*; his huge success with it remained the main element of his career, while his view of looking at art became part of public discourse. Many of his other publishing endeavors, however, are of equal importance.

Landscapes (2016) and its companion volume, *Portraits: John Berger on Artists* (2015), are the best summation to date of Berger's career as a critic. *Landscapes* runs the historical gamut of art from the prehistoric cave paintings of Lascaux* to the work of modern artists unknown to the wider public. To read it is to be reminded of two of Berger's unique virtues: the clarity of his writing and his unique focus on each artist's way of looking. What *Landscapes* makes clear, "is that Berger is a rigorous thinker with a theory of art. That theory evolved considerably between the 1950s and 2010s. Yet two threads hold it together with the tenacity of spider silk: a critique of the political economy of art and a sophisticated account of its human value, each rooted in a committed but elastic Marxism."[2]

Regardless of the era he studies or the decade in which he writes, his lyrical prose always ultimately serves a fervent political concern. From the beginning of his professional career, Berger has maintained a high—"some might argue nearly impossible—pedagogical standard for visual art. Writing in the 1960s as the critic for the *New Statesman*, Berger famously staked his claim: 'Does this work help or encourage men to know and claim their social rights?' That seminal question … can be detected in nearly all of the writing in *Portraits* … In Jean-Francois Millet,* he sees an admirable man that strove to live and breathe the arduous life of a peasant."[3] In accordance with his Marxist views, Berger's book on *The Success and failure of Picasso* appeared in 1965, where he set about to demythologize the "man of genius" approach taken by many Picasso scholars at that time. Berger demonstrated a dualism in the phenomenon of Picasso: while society appraised him as a genius with all the mystery that entails, his art became a bourgeois commodity that the artist realized and successfully took advantage of in his own lifetime.

Significance

Berger's most influential essays deal with the representation of females in art, which have now been explored further by feminist art theory. The author's work has also helped to shape a relatively new academic field, that of visual culture. This discipline draws on different subjects, such as history of art, cultural studies, anthropology, and philosophy, and focuses on aspects of culture that rely on visual images. The essay in which Berger talks about the concept of women and their depiction in art (as he argues that they are commonly objectified and painted in a way to be admired by their male audience) has assumed great importance in developing the concept of the "male gaze." This essay, along with work by Laura Mulvey* and Griselda Pollock, is considered hugely influential in this field.

Berger's importance in the development of new theories is evidenced in the fact that scholars have adapted the original ideas of the text and customized them. One critic sums up the impact by stating: "Berger's materialistic views on culture had enormous resonance in the field of cultural production. Writers on representations of women have used Berger's ideas in a variety of ways … both on advertising and … on women's magazines."[4]

As *Ways of Seeing* is still a relatively new seminal text, it is hard to identify any particular schools of thought in the ideas it contains. One thing that can be established with certainty, however, is the fact that it has inspired and challenged academics of many different disciplines, and continues to do so. A general search on the Internet will reveal many academic publications that use Berger's ideas as a "jumping off point" for constructing new arguments on the themes he discusses. Even though these do not always agree with Berger's initial ideas, they often use his terminology to expand and explore the arguments further.

NOTES

1 Quoted in Sean O'Hagan, "A Radical Returns," *The Guardian*, (April 03, 2005), accessed June 19, 2017, https://www.theguardian.com/artanddesign/2005/apr/03/art.art1.

2 See Robert Minto, "A Smuggling Operation: John Berger's Theory of Art," *Los Angeles Review of Books* (January 2, 2017), accessed June 25, 2017, https://lareviewofbooks.org/article/a-smuggling-operation-john-bergers-theory-of-art/.

3 Sara Christoph, "Portraits: John Berger on Artists," *The Brooklyn Rail* (February 3, 2016), accessed June 25, 2017, http://brooklynrail.org/2016/02/art_books/john-berger-on-artists.

4 Mike Edwards, *Key Ideas in Media* (Cheltenham, Glos.: Nelson Thornes, 2003), 62.

MODULE 9
THE FIRST RESPONSES

KEY POINTS

- While the work received a lot of publicity, some critics did not look upon *Ways of Seeing* fondly.

- Some might say that this controversy is exactly what Berger was trying to achieve: to start a process of questioning.

- While some of Berger's contemporaries (such as Fuller) later revised their opinions, Berger maintained his views and remained true to his politics.

Criticism

When John Berger's *Ways of Seeing* was first published, it prompted sharply different reactions. In some quarters it created outrage, with some critics dismissing many of the arguments Berger made and accusing him of provoking and exaggerating, which is arguably what he was trying to achieve. On the broadcasting of the television series *Ways of Seeing* in 1972, the *Guardian's* art critic Norbert Lynton, accused Berger of debasing the classics: "I often cannot believe Berger … it is clear from his writings that he is a sensitive man and in many ways a wise one, and that he is willing to lie about art to make his political points."[1] In a wide-ranging 2002 essay in the *London Review of Books* responding to Berger's *Selected Essays*, Peter Wollen also accused Berger of imagining art only in "conventionally optical terms," to such an extent that "much of the art of 20th century has passed him by."[2] In *Educating for Art*, Rod Taylor also reports on the tragic influence *Ways of Seeing* has had in the nation's schools [by undermining] art teacher's attitudes to gallery visiting. "Predictably, *Ways of Seeing* has not given

> **❝ Nothing** demonstrates how Berger's radical prospectus for the arts ... has become the philistine and reactionary reality ... more than the case of Gilbert and George* ... The then burgeoning conceptual art movement, which seemed to have taken his advice quite literally ... abandoned traditional painting and sculpture ... and produced works which (apparently) could not be bought and sold. **❞**
>
> Peter Fuller,* *Seeing Through Berger*

rise to any 'alternative form of art appreciation'; that is hardly possible when pupils are separated from any direct contact with works of art."[3]

The art critic Peter Fuller was one of those who severely criticized *Ways of Seeing*. Berger, he says, "has written numerous essays, of great brilliance ... which have not assumed that the fundamental fact of the artist's vision and practice was a relationship to property. This should, perhaps, have caused one to question some of the arguments of *Ways of Seeing*."[4] Overall, this attack was based not only on the idea of a fully materialist theory of expression that was missing from Berger's account of the Hals painting[5] or on the fact that *Ways of Seeing* has nothing to say about sculpture,[6] but also on Fuller's belief—in contrast to Berger—that paintings and photographs are very different sorts of things. According to Fuller, "photography is much closer to being a mechanical record of a way of seeing than painting." Therefore, while "photography is merely process ... painting is not like this at all."[7]

Fuller may be right in at least one respect: *Ways of Seeing* was not merely influential in the realm of theory, it was also even more influential in the realm of artistic practice. As John Walker explains: "Fine artists in Britain and North America were encouraged by Berger's analysis to undertake their own critiques of mass media images and to use them to make critical photo-montages, films, photo text and slide-tape works, and posters. At the same time, Berger cannot be blamed for the political and moral content of the photo-murals and films of artists like Gilbert and George ... Once any knowledge [is] produced by a theorist ... it can be utilized by artists of various political persuasions ..."[8] Despite all that, the critics' outrage over some of the concepts does not undermine the consensus view of the text, but may in fact have fueled more interest in the book.

Responses

John Berger's initial response to criticism of *Ways of Seeing* is directed to the criticism made by Peter Fuller, who had previously been a friend. In 1980 Fuller wrote a book about Berger, entitled *Seeing Berger*,[9] which served as a re-evaluation of *Ways of Seeing*. Although the book contains praise, it soon launches into mild criticism of Berger's concept and hints at the fact that his ideas are polemical and partial—Fuller accuses Berger of overstating his case. In 1988 the controversies aroused by *Ways of Seeing* were re-opened when Fuller recanted his earlier opinions and attacked the series for what he regarded as its negative influence on contemporary art and values. It was Berger's director, Mike Dibb, however, who responded directly to Fuller's criticism. "To suggest as you do ..." Dibb says, "is ludicrous. We never said that advertising was the modern version of art. What we did try to suggest was that many of the pictorial *codes* of European painting now find a regular ... place within advertising, with colour photography even more than oil painting providing a means for rendering the physical world ever more tactile and desirable ... And frankly I cannot believe that art teachers and their students could seriously be undermined by it. It is not a sacrosanct book, just one to be used, together with much else."[10]

Berger also responded openly to some of his critics in a later edition of *Ways of Seeing*. In the case of Professor Lawrence Gowing, he starts an open feud concerning the painting of Mr and Mrs Andrews by Gainsborough, by quoting a comment he had received from the professor. In this comment Berger is accused of "interposing himself between us and the visible meaning of a good picture"[11] before arguing his point about the subject of ownership in the painting. Following this quotation, Berger encourages his audience to question Gowing's argument, calling it "an illustration of the disingenuousness that bedevils the subject of art history."[12]

Upon closer inspection of Berger's critics, however, we can learn that these were often highly educated and came from a privileged background. They often epitomized the "cultural establishment" Berger fought against, and this may have fueled their criticism of the author and his work in an attempt to defend the cultural establishment.

Conflict And Consensus

The text was revolutionary in that it went against convention, and challenged the values and principles upheld by the "cultural establishment." There were, however, art critics who would identify with Berger's ideas, such as, initially, Peter Fuller.[13] In his early work, Fuller praises *Ways of Seeing* and its ideas, and even points out what an inspiration Berger had been to him. In his later work, however, he retracts his position, accusing Berger of dishonesty in his treatment of Clark's work. This feud is also said to have sparked "an unholy, anti-aesthetic alliance between certain intellectuals of both left and right."[14] John Walker provides a good overview and rightly states that a whole book would be needed to explore the feud between Berger and Fuller.[15]

One of Berger's most immediate responses to criticism can be found in an interview he gave in the mid-1980s. "The weakness of *Ways of Seeing*," he says, "is that I didn't create a theory of the exceptional work of art, that I didn't go further in explaining a mystery which I felt *was* there in paintings …"[16] However, he believed that *Ways of Seeing* could not be revised and brought up to date. When recently asked by the BBC to "revisit" the original television series of *Ways of Seeing*, which formed the basis for the book, he declined. Michael Dibb, director and co-author of *Ways of Seeing*, also admitted in a recent interview that there was not much he would want to change.[17]

NOTES

1   Ben Davis, "The Unfinished Business of John Berger," *Artnet* (January 6, 2017), accessed June 24, 2017, https://news.artnet.com/art-world/the-unfinished-business-of-john-berger-806741.

2   Davis, "The Unfinished Business of John Berger."

3   Peter Fuller, *Seeing Through Berger* (London: The Claridge Press, 1988), 63.

4   Fuller, *Seeing Through Berger*, 17.

5   Fuller, *Seeing Through Berger*, 25.

6   Fuller, *Seeing Through Berger*, 34–7.

7   Fuller, *Seeing Through Berger*, 27–8.

8   John Walker, *Arts TV: A History of Arts Television in Britain* (London: John Libbey, 1993), 115.

9   Peter Fuller, *Seeing Berger: A Re-evaluation of* Ways of Seeing (London: Writers and Readers, 1980).

10 Fuller, *Seeing Through Berger*, 69–74.

11 John Berger, *Ways of Seeing* (London: Penguin, 2008), 108.

12 Berger, *Ways of Seeing*, 108.

13 Peter Fuller, "The Value of Art," *New Society*, Jan 29, 1988.

14 Richard Howells and Joaquim Negreiros, *Visual Culture*, 2nd ed. (Cambridge: Polity Press, 2012), 93.

15 Walker, *Arts TV*, 101.

16 "Ways of Witnessing," Interview with John Berger, *Marxism Today* (December 1984), 36–37 (PDF), accessed June 25, 2017, http://www.unz.org/Pub/MarxismToday-1984dec-00036.

17 Juliette Kristensen, "Making *Ways of Seeing*: A Conversation with Mike Dibb and Richard Hollis," *Journal of Visual Culture* 11:2 (August 2012): 181–95.

MODULE 10
THE EVOLVING DEBATE

KEY POINTS

- *Ways of Seeing* has had an effect on several intellectual movements, most of which had not quite taken shape at the time of its writing.

- The ideas presented in *Ways of Seeing* have been dissected, and informed new ways of thinking beyond the field of art criticism.

- *Ways of Seeing* had a deep impact on several major intellectual figures, including recent thinkers, such as Adrian Barlow* and Amelia Jones.*

Uses And Problems

To a certain extent, it is possible to trace the influence of *Ways of Seeing* in the subsequent evolution of art history. Berger's ideas have inspired a new way of looking at art and created an intellectual field from which figures such as T. J. Clark and Griselda Pollock have emerged. Berger's work has also formed an important contribution to the field of visual culture, a discipline that overlaps with other fields focused on aspects of culture reliant on visual imagery. Furthermore, it has impacted second-wave feminism, which started to gain momentum in the 1960s and 1970s. In his essay, Berger argues the role of women from a feminist point of view, drawing attention to the fact that "men act and women appear,"[1] illustrating his point with a range of examples drawn from the tradition of European oil painting. Another area in which the work's influence is discernible is the field of media studies as one of the essays in the book offers a new perspective on advertising. Here, controversially,

> **❝** There can be few intentions so abundantly fulfilled, as the readers—and lookers—who have continued to pose questions about sight and its vicissitudes have been legion. Future historians will, in fact likely date the launch of visual culture studies as a serious scholarly field of study to the publication of *Ways of Seeing.* **❞**
>
> Martin Jay, "Ways of Seeing at Forty," Journal of Visual Culture

Berger makes the link between oil painting and modern media, such as photography, stating that "colour photography is to the spectator-buyer what oil paint was to the spectator-owner."[2]

Some would argue that Berger's impact is not just limited to theory, but has also influenced practical aspects of the discipline of art.[3] Berger's impact is discernible across different disciplines within the broad field of visual culture, and the book's contribution is evident in different subjects, ranging from art history to studies on media, film, culture, and photography, to mention but a few. In terms of its application, the text can be described as a "game-changer" in that it discusses Western art in a unique and accessible way that does not cater only to elite audiences, challenging many of the previously held assumptions about paintings by Old Masters . The fact that *Ways of Seeing* first aired as a television series, before being turned into a book, contributed to its success in reaching a wider audience.

Schools Of Thought

Over the past 40 years John Berger's *Ways of Seeing* has inspired academics and scholars from a wide range of disciplines. One could argue that Berger has achieved his main objective, which was to start a process of questioning. He has accomplished this by bringing new ideas to our consciousness, such as the objectification of women in art, which in turn gave birth to a new set of theories and ideas, informing our understanding of new subjects, including feminism—his ideas were broadcast at a time when the feminist movement was starting to take shape. Griselda Pollock argues that it was Berger's *Ways of Seeing* that "inexplicably and effortlessly exploded the aura the institutions of art history fabricated and allowed the visual arts to become interesting if not significant locations for analysis of power and the deconstruction of classed, raced, and gendered meanings."[4] It is difficult to know whether Berger would have understood all of these new applications at the time of writing. Some of them might have come as a surprise to him, considering the wide range of subjects on which the book has had an impact over the past four decades. It has even been cited as a reference in publications on video games.[5] Some works can be seen not only as a continuation of Berger's ideas, but also as a kind of evolution.

In Current Scholarship

Ways of Seeing is central to the intellectual world of many academics who have been influenced by Berger's ideas, and have subsequently developed them or applied them to other disciplines. The degree to which these scholars have remained true to Berger's original text has varied greatly. Some may have taken Berger's ideas as a starting point, using it to construct their own meaning. Adrian Barlow, for example, the author of *World and Time: Teaching Literature in Context*, has developed Berger's argument about representations of women in art and applied it to the subject of literature.[6] In his work he talks openly about how Berger inspired him and how he applied the author's methods and discussions to his own work. Barlow draws some obvious parallels with *Ways of Seeing*, but develops some of its ideas, resituating them in a contemporary context and within a different field. Art historian and critic Amelia Jones has also used Berger's book as a key text in developing the argument of the "male gaze" further within the discipline of feminism and visual culture.[7]

Berger's comments on the role of women gave birth to a generation of new theories on feminism and have made a great contribution to our understanding of the concept of the "male gaze" and politics of gender.[8] Equally important is Berger's essay on photography and advertising, voicing political views on consumerism. His ideas have influenced scholars on subjects such as anthropology, history, film, and photography, impacting on media criticism and even led to the creation of a new field, visual culture. Many have either briefly touched upon his ideas, borrowing his terminology, or completely revisited his arguments and explored them in more depth. It is difficult, however, to identify individual scholars that can be considered devoted followers of Berger's ideas in *Ways of Seeing*. While the text's influence can be felt in the work of art historians, cultural historians, and literary and Marxist theorists, it is usually as a pioneering reference tool for carrying out a literary reading of mass culture, rather than as an ongoing academic project.[9]

NOTES

1   John Berger, *Ways of Seeing* (London: Penguin, 2008), 47.

2   Berger, *Ways of Seeing*, 140.

3   John Walker, *Arts TV: A History of Arts Television in Britain* (London: John Libbey, 1993), 100.

4   Griselda Pollock, "Muscular Defences," *Journal of Visual Culture* 11: 2 (August 2012): 127–31, 127.

5   Peter Bell, "Realism and subjectivity in first-person shooter video games," *Journal of Communication, Culture and Technology* (2003), accessed July 25, 2017, http://www.gnovisjournal.org/files/Peter-Bell-Realism-and-Subjectivity.pdf.

6   Adrian Barlow, *World and Time: Teaching Literature in Context* (Cambridge: Cambridge University Press, 2009).

7   Amelia Jones, ed., *The Feminism and Visual Culture Reader* (New York: Routledge, 2003).

8   See, for example, Heather Rogers, "Still Seeing: Berger's Critique of High
    Art Turns 30," *The Brooklyn Rail: Critical Perspectives on Arts, Politics
    and Culture* (Autumn 2002), accessed April 27, 2013, http://brooklynrail.
    org/2002/10/books/still-seeing-bergers-critique-of-high-ar [sic].

9   For the extent to which scholars have taken the cross-disciplinary model of
    Ways of Seeing as a "distant inspiration", see, for instance, Marita Sturken,
    "Ways of Seeing, Practices of Looking," *Journal of Visual Culture* 11:2
    (August 2012): 151–53.

IMPACT AND INFLUENCE TODAY

KEY POINTS

- The content of visual culture, mass media, and image reproduction has changed, but *Ways of Seeing* remains as important as ever.
- Many of Berger's insights are still as true for contemporary consumption of culture as they were in the early 1970s.
- As visual culture continues to have a powerful influence on society, modern re-workings of *Ways of Seeing* update his message.

Position

Even though this work was first published in 1972, many ideas still stand up today, which is why *Ways of Seeing* is still considered a key undergraduate text. With respect to his thoughts on media and photography, many of Berger's ideas are still being explored further by academics, and critically analyzed in journals and research papers. This continual reworking of Berger's themes forms part of the evidence that *Ways of Seeing* continues to challenge and transform existing ideas. The fact that the book remains in print also supports these claims. The book is on many compulsory reading lists in art or media studies, now assuming the status of a "classic" (and published by the *Penguin Classics* imprint). Some themes, however, have become more outdated. The Marxist tone, for example, a key aspect of *Ways of Seeing*, found appeal with many groups in the late 1960s and early 1970s, but has become less important nowadays with a change in politics toward a more conservative view (although there are still practicing Marxist art critics today).

> **"** I don't think there's anything in *Ways of Seeing*
> that's dated ... I think there are arguments in it which
> have been refined and developed, but ... most of the
> arguments ... are still incredibly strong and still speak to
> the world we live in now. **"**
>
> Mike Dibb, Sunday Morning—Radio National

For a collection of essays dedicated to analyzing the way we appreciate and look at paintings back in 1972, *Ways of Seeing* feels surprisingly contemporary. The spread of pop culture and digital media has brought renewed freshness to the debate, and Berger's principal message remains as powerful as ever. *Ways of Seeing* has been absorbed so fully into the current intellectual climate that it is possible to overlook just how prophetic Berger's vision was. According to Clive Dilnot,* there are four obvious characteristics of the book that have enabled this resilience and contributed to its undoubted success. First, it is an exemplary pedagogical work, perhaps the greatest we have in its field. Second, *Ways of Seeing* offers a unique and original format. Third, the book possesses an enviable transparency of argument. Finally, more essential to the book's success than is usually acknowledged, is the affirmative and declarative rhythm of Berger's sentences;"a cadence that feels close to spoken language."[1]

Interaction

The book has unexpected relevance today, especially in terms of media or culture studies. In one of his essays, Berger establishes a controversial link between oil painting and advertising, doing so by looking at consumerist society and publicity photographs. While some of the specific advertising images to which he refers have now dated, this point has even more relevance today, as the advance in media technology has increased the exposure to such imagery. Our society is more dominated than ever by publicity images, encouraging people to embrace consumerism.

The book was criticized mainly for its omissions or inconsistencies, and sometimes accused of overstating its case.[2] The same could still be argued today, as a critic exploring Berger's book 30 years later notes: "Compared to those who are currently on the cutting edge of socially aware art criticism, Berger's book seems dated in its narrow focus and lack of attention to institutions like museums, criticism and art education."[3] On the other hand, however, Berger had paved the way for critics to explore his ideas and add to the fields of study he touches upon. Douglas Kellner,* for example, builds on Berger's work and explores critical perspectives on visual imagery in media and cyber culture.*[4] Stephanie O'Donohue*[5] presents another example of where Burger's ideas are used to help shape an argument on attitudes relating to advertising in post-modern times. In her paper she argues that although research on attitudes to advertising has generally focused on the attitudes themselves at the expense of contextual factors, consumers do not relate to advertising in isolation from their experiences of popular culture, postmodernism, and advertising literacy.

Although art historical research has taken different directions—largely because of Berger himself—since the 1970s, it is difficult not to think of Berger in a huge number of modern contexts. There is no doubt that *Ways of Seeing* might still be a significant guide to the endless possibilities of social media challenging scholars to find new and intelligent ways to think and write about art history and visual culture. By exposing the power dynamics beneath the innocent surface of an image, Berger might not have anticipated the extent to which technology has so democratized image-making that the power to own an image once associated with a privileged few is now owned by everyone. Thus, when we think "of the mixed feelings inspired by Instagram's* effortlessly artful images … [we also] think of Berger writing about the politics of 'glamour'."[6] Indeed, the book's relevance as a way of thinking about social media angst is clear: "Glamour cannot exist without social envy being a common and widespread emotion ... The pursuit of individual happiness has been acknowledged as a universal right. Yet the existing social conditions make the individual feel powerless. He lives in contradiction between what he is and what he would like to be."[7]

The Continuing Debate

Certain themes discussed in John Berger's *Ways of Seeing* continue to be part of current intellectual debate. His assertions on topics such as the "male gaze" have been looked at particularly in connection with female representations in a range of media. Moreover, Berger's Marxist art history and criticism set in motion partly by him in the 1960s, never ceased to inform and affect academic scholarship and art criticism. In the *Aesthetic of* Power, Carol Duncan* exposes art criticism by arguing that official writing about art adds value to it, making it sell for more on the market. As in *Ways of Seeing*, Duncan believes that this selective privilege of the art object not only ensures the monetary value of the work, but it also creates a wall between "high art" and the rest. Art is now defined by what the art establishment says it is, whatever art critics write about, whatever art experts teach, whatever is hung in galleries. "This is a very convenient and profitable model for the establishment ... [which] would never forgive Berger for evolving a theory of art which told the world that the art mafia is actually just 'the cultural hierarchy of relic specialists.'"[8] While Berger did not focus on contemporary art market, he led the way for a new art criticism, more radical than ever before, that Duncan and others continue to develop.

Because of social media and the Internet, people have come closer to culture and art objects than ever before. These constant developments have encouraged many people to visit museums and exhibitions increasing the first-hand experience of works of art. However, the mediating factor should not be forgotten. Screen images of paintings, sculpture and architecture are—and will always be—second-hand representations. Whether the continual exposure to this kind of imagery ruins the capacity to appreciate paintings or sculptures is hard to judge. Digital and television images, however, are a powerful presence, and this would have come as no surprise to Berger.

NOTES

1   Clive Dilnot, "Seven Characteristics of *Ways of Seeing,*" *Journal of Visual Culture* 11:2 (August 2012): 148–51.

2   Richard Howells and Joaquim Negreiros, *Visual Culture*, 2nd ed. (Cambridge: Polity Press, 2012), 93.

3   Heather Rogers, "Still Seeing: Berger's Critique of High Art Turns 30," *The Brooklyn Rail: Critical Perspectives on Arts, Politics and Culture* (Autumn 2002), accessed May 30, 2013, http://brooklynrail.org/2002/10/books/still-seeing-bergers-critique-of-high-ar.

4   Douglas Kellner, "Critical Perspectives on Visual Imagery in Media and Cyberculture," *Journal of Visual Literacy*, 22:1 (Spring 2002).

5   Stephanie O'Donohoe, "Living with Ambivalence: Attitudes to Advertising in Postmodern Times," *Marketing Theory* 1:1 (March 2001), 91–108.

6   See Ben Davis, "Ways of Seeing Instagram" (June 24, 2014), accessed July 4, 2017, https://news.artnet.com/exhibitions/ways-of-seeing-instagram-37635.

7   John Berger, *Ways of Seeing* (London: Penguin, 2008), 148.

8   Bob Light, "John Berger Opened Up New Ways of Seeing," *Socialist Review* (February 2017): 421, accessed June 20, 2017, http://socialistreview.org.uk/421/john-berger-opened-new-ways-seeing.

MODULE 12
WHERE NEXT?

KEY POINTS

- *Ways of Seeing* is likely to remain an influential text because it helps all sorts of viewers to understand and appreciate visual culture.

- *Ways of Seeing* will continue to stimulate debate as it deals with themes that are still explored in modern-day society.

- With *Ways of Seeing* Berger achieved his main mission: he started a process of questioning, which is likely to continue for some time.

Potential

What place does John Berger's *Ways of Seeing* occupy in our lives today? *Ways of Seeing* works as a mode of cultural encounter; a way of looking at art and interpreting the images that surround us in our daily lives. This approach holds the potential to continually be renewed in relation to new social media and cultural landscapes. The reproduction of the visual arts today is full of fresh contradictions of distributing images in much more varied ways than before, and for this reason *Ways of Seeing* will remain a key reference point. It is possible that changes and developments in future years will reshape some of the arguments made within the book, especially with regard to advertising and increased exposure to images. The fact that *Ways of Seeing* is still in print 45 years after it was first published probably best demonstrates the text's continuing relevance. Even though many things have changed in recent decades, the text is still living and significant. For this reason, it remains compulsory on many

> 66 It is, however, vital to acknowledge the undeniable impact of a work that advanced a strong and unapologetic argument confuting the prevailing wisdom of its day, and yet somehow was able to find a mass television audience and then became a canonical text for a generation. 99
>
> Martin Jay, "Ways of Seeing at Forty." Journal of Visual Culture

reading lists for art courses, as its ideas are considered to be of great value and importance. Overall, it is likely that Berger's seminal text will be enduringly influential in the future and form the basis for many debates and discussions to come.

Future Directions

Some of the key ideas outlined in *Ways of Seeing* are discernible in current discussions in media, visual culture, film, photography, feminism and even literature. It is likely that Berger's ideas will, directly or indirectly, go on to evolve and influence new generations of scholars in years to come. One area in which the text's core ideas may be further developed is in relation to image reproduction. The Internet, in particular, will continue to contribute greatly to the mass reproduction of images to consumers across the globe. Instead of just looking at it, consumers today participate directly in the creation and dissemination of culture—in terms of visual arts—in real time offering comments and analyses through interactive platforms such as blogs, comment sections, forums, and other social media sites; a world unimaginable four decades before. Moreover, the individual essays of the book do not read as mere examples of an old-fashioned mode of cultural or art criticism, but, instead, have the potential to remain persuasive in a way that ensures that the collection can be read as more than a product of its own time. For students, this opens up enormous possibilities, as the guiding impulse and critical edge can be taken forward endlessly, encouraging a much broader scope for looking at art and culture.

Summary

Although *Ways of Seeing* is considered one of the author's important works, John Berger is a key literary figure, and this is not the only text by him that deserves scholarly attention. Berger has also published a number of other influential works. He is an acclaimed author who has written essays on a wide range of topics. Furthermore, he is highly regarded as an author of works of fiction, the most important of which is arguably the novel *G.*, for which he won the Booker Prize in 1972, the same year that *Ways of Seeing* was published. However, it is the latter that deserves special attention as it has made a vital contribution to several different disciplines.

Ways of Seeing can be considered an original and pioneering text in a number of ways. Its formatting and style are as innovative as the themes contained within, although some have been met with huge controversy. Berger's attack on bourgeois society and his unconventional linkage of ideas—establishing a relationship between the tradition of European oil painting and modern advertising, for example—have not only sparked many debates, but also impacted on different disciplines. To a certain extent, Berger's thinking initiated a move toward a social art history, by considering the historical and social context of a work of art in art criticism. This text is significant and revolutionary as it was a major departure from art criticism commonly practiced at the time. Its clear, direct and very accessible style of writing, as well as its equally outspoken preceding television series, meant that it was successful in reaching a wide audience. It addressed the general public in a direct manner, encouraging them to look at art in a new way. It confronted the public, urging people to "see" paintings, to study them in depth, and then form their own judgment.

GLOSSARY OF TERMS

Aesthetics: a branch of philosophy concerned with the evaluation of beauty.

Aura: a subtly pervasive quality or atmosphere that seems to surround and be generated by a person, thing, or place.

Black Panther Party (BPP): a revolutionary black nationalist and socialist organization founded by Bobby Seale and Huey Newton in October 1966 in Oakland, California.

Booker McConnel Prize (commonly referred to as as the Booker Prize and now known as the Man Booker Prize) is a literary prize awarded each year for the best original novel, written in the English language and published in the UK.

Bourgeoisie: a social order made up of the middle classes. In social and political theory, the term is used by Marxists to describe the social class that monopolizes the benefits of modernization to the detriment of the proletariat.

British realism: the tradition of social realism in British film (see social realism).

Capitalism: an economic system dominant in the Western world since the break-up of feudalism, in which most of the means of production are privately owned and production is guided and income distributed through the operation of markets.

Civil rights movements: a mass protest movement against racial segregation and discrimination in the southern United States that came to national prominence during the mid-1950s.

Cavilling: captious objection or frivolous fault-finding (OED).

Cold War (1947–91): period of high political tension from roughly 1947 to 1991 between the Western bloc, a group of countries including the United States and its European allies, and the Eastern bloc, a group of countries including the Soviet Union and its European allies.

Commonwealth of Nations: also known as simply the Commonwealth, is an intergovernmental organization of 52 member states that are mostly former territories of the British Empire.

Conceptual art: art for which the idea (or concept) behind the work is more important than the finished art object. It emerged as an art movement in the 1960s and the term usually refers to art made from the mid-1960s to the mid-1970s.

Connoisseur: a person who has a great deal of knowledge about fine arts, or is an expert judge in matters of taste.

Consumerism: a social and economic order and ideology that encourages the acquisition of goods and services in ever increasing amounts.

Cyber culture or computer culture: the culture that has emerged, or is emerging, from the use of computer networks for communication, entertainment, and business.

Dutch Golden Age: a period in Dutch history, roughly spanning the seventeenth century, in which Dutch trade, science, military, and art were among the most acclaimed in the world.

Ecological art: an art genre and artistic practice that seeks to preserve, remediate, and/or vitalize the life forms, resources and ecology of Earth. It is distinct from environmental art, which addresses social and political issues relating to the natural and urban environment.

Elitism: the belief or attitude that a society or system should be led by an elite.

Feminism: a political movement concerned with defending equal rights for women. Whereas the first wave, between the late nineteenth and early twentieth centuries, was primarily concerned with women's legal rights and especially women's suffrage, second-wave feminism attacked and sought to remedy *de facto* socio-cultural inequalities and perceptions.

Feminist art: art by women artists made consciously in the light of developments in feminist art theory in the early 1970s.

Fresco: a method of painting water-based pigments on freshly applied plaster, usually on wall surfaces.

Gender politics: the debate about the roles and relations of men and women.

Genre painting: a category of paintings that depict scenes of everyday life.

High culture: a set of cultural products of aesthetic value, mainly in the arts, held in the highest esteem by an elite.

Ideology: a system of beliefs or principles that aspire to explain the world or change it.

Instagram: a mobile and Internet-based photo-sharing application and service that allows users to share pictures and videos either publicly or privately.

Kitchen sink painters: a term applied to a group of British artists working in the 1950s who painted ordinary people in scenes of everyday life.

Landscape painting: one of the principal types or genres of subject in Western art.

Left-wing: sympathetic toward the left in politics.

Male gaze: the way in which the visual arts and literature depict the world and women from a masculine point of view, presenting women as objects of male pleasure.

Marxism: a worldview and form of socio-economic inquiry rooted in the economic theory of the nineteenth-century economist and political theorist Karl Marx and industrialist Friedrich Engels.

Materialist: a person who supports the theory that nothing exists except matter and its movements and modifications.

May 1968: the volatile period of civil unrest in France during May 1968 that was punctuated by demonstrations and massive general strikes as well as the occupation of universities and factories across France.

Modern art: artistic work produced during the period extending roughly from the 1860s to the 1970s, and denotes the style and philosophy of the art produced during that era.

Objectification: the demotion or degrading of a person or class of people (especially women) to the status of a mere object.

Old Masters: the term usually refers to the most recognized and skilled artists—mostly painters—working between the Renaissance and 1800.

Performance art: artworks that are created through actions performed by the artist or other participants, which may be live or recorded, spontaneous or scripted.

Political economy: a term used for studying production and trade, and their relations with law, custom, and government, as well as with the distribution of national income and wealth.

Post-modernism: a reaction against modernism (in art), which had dominated art theory and practice since the beginning of the twentieth century. The term post-modernism is also widely used to describe challenges and changes to established structures and belief systems that took place in Western society and culture from the 1960s onwards.

Renaissance: a period in European history, from the fourteenth to the seventeenth century, regarded as the cultural bridge between the Middle Ages and modern history.

Ruling class: the social class of a given society that decides upon and sets that society's political agenda

Social art history: highly influential movement widely practiced by art historians, particularly during the 1980s and 1990s. Although it assumes less importance today, it still holds some relevance, as it presented a new perspective on looking at art.

Social humanist tradition: see socialist (Marxist) humanism.

Social realism: an international art movement, encompassing the work of painters, printmakers, photographers, and filmmakers who draw attention to the everyday conditions of the working class and the poor.

Socialist (Marxist) humanism: a branch of Marxism that primarily focuses on Marx's earlier writings in which Marx espoused his theory of alienation, as opposed to his later works, which are considered to be concerned more with his structural conception of capitalist society.

Sociology: the scientific study of the development, structure, and functioning of human society.

Video art: an art form that relies on moving pictures in a visual and audio medium.

Vietnam War (1954–75): a protracted conflict that pitted the communist government of North Vietnam and its allies in South Vietnam, against the government of South Vietnam and its principal ally, the United States.

West Indies: a former federation (1958–62) of the British islands in the Caribbean, comprising Barbados, Jamaica, Trinidad, Tobago, and the Windward and Leeward Island colonies.

Women's liberation movement: a series of political campaigns for reforms on issues such as domestic violence, maternity leave, equal pay, sexual harassment, and sexual violence, all of which fall under the label of feminism and the feminist movement.

PEOPLE MENTIONED IN THE TEXT

Theodor W. Adorno (1903–69) was one of the leading philosophers of the Frankfurt School of critical theory. He made significant contribution to the intellectual fields of philosophy, musicology, aesthetics, and sociology.

Frederick Antal (1887–1954) was Jewish Hungarian Marxist art historian. He is best known for his contributions to the social history of art.

Adrian Barlow is the president of the English Association, series editor of "Cambridge Contexts in Literature" and former Director of Public and Professional Programmes at Cambridge University Institute of Continuing Education.

Walter Benjamin (1892–1940) was a German literary critic and essayist associated with the Frankfurt School of social theorists who is regarded one of the most important intellectual figures of the twentieth century. He is best known for his essay "The Work of Art in the Age of Mechanical Reproduction" (1936).

Adriaen Brouwer (1605–38) was a Flemish painter. He was an important innovator of the genre painting and his sheer talent and flair for human comedy earned him the esteem of Rubens and Rembrandt.

Albert Camus (1913–60) was a French philosopher, author, and journalist. His views contributed to the philosophy known as absurdism (the conflict between the human tendency to seek inherent value and meaning in life and the human inability to find any).

Ferdinand Cheval (1836–1924) was a French postman who spent thirty-three years of his life building Le Palais idéal in Hauterives. The Palace is regarded as an extraordinary example of naïve art architecture.

Kenneth Clark (1903–83) was a famous English art historian and museum director. He was the author and presenter of the influential television series *Civilisation*, which was also published in the form of a book.

Timothy James "T. J." Clark (b. 1943) is a British art historian and writer. He has been influential in developing the field of art history, examining modern paintings as an articulation of the social and political conditions of modern life.

Leonardo da Vinci (1452–1519) was an Italian Renaissance artist and polymath. He is widely considered among the greatest painters of all time.

Mike Dibb (b. 1940) is an award-winning English documentary filmmaker. In a career spanning almost five decades, he made films on subjects including cinema, literature, art, jazz, sport, and popular culture defining the televisual art documentary genre.

Clive Dilnot is Professor of Design Studies in the School of Art and Design History and Theory at Parsons. His teaching and writing have focused on design history, theory and criticism.

Carol Duncan is an art historian specializing in the history of museums in the United States. She is the author of numerous books and articles on the subject.

Geoff Dyer (b. 1958) is an English writer and journalist. He has published a critical study of John Berger entitled *Ways of Telling* and has also edited Berger's *Selected Essays*.

Ernst Fischer (1899–1972) was a Bohemian-born Austrian journalist, writer, and politician. He is particularly famous for his book *The Necessity of Art* (1959) where he discusses Marxist theories and art history.

Peter Fuller (1947–90) was a highly educated British art critic and editor. He was originally a friend and follower of John Berger, but their relationship broke down as his political viewpoint changed.

Thomas Gainsborough (1727–88) was an English portrait and landscape painter, draftsman, and printmaker. Together with Sir Joshua Reynolds (his main rival) he was the leading portrait painter in England in the later eighteenth century.

Gilbert (b. 1943) and George (b. 1942) are two artists who work together as a collaborative art duo. They are known for their distinctive and highly formal appearance and manner in performance art.

Ernst Gombrich (1909–2001) was an Austrian-born art historian who spent most of his working life in the United Kingdom. He was the author of *The Story of Art*, a book widely regarded as one of the most accessible introductions to the visual arts.

Sir Lawrence Gowing (1918–91) was an artist and writer. He was a prominent figure in the field of arts education and also worked as a curator.

Frans Hals the Elder (1580–1666) was a Dutch Golden Age portrait painter who lived and worked in Haarlem. He is notable for his loose painterly brushwork, helping introduce this lively style of painting into Dutch art.

Arnold Hauser (1892–1978) was a Hungarian art historian. He was among the leading Marxists in the field and wrote on the influence of change in social structures on art.

Hans Holbein the Younger (1497–1543) was a German artist and printmaker who worked in a Northern Renaissance style mainly in Basel and London. He is best known as one of the greatest portraitists of the 16th century.

Amelia Jones (b. 1961) is an American art historian, art critic, and curator specializing in feminist art, body/performance art, video art and Dadaism. She is currently the Robert A. Day Chair in Art and Design at the Roski School of Art and Design at the University of Southern California.

Douglas Kellner (b. 1943) early theorist of the field of critical media literacy and has been a leading theorist of media culture generally. He is currently the George Kneller Chair in the Philosophy of Education in the Graduate School of Education and Information Studies at the University of California, Los Angeles.

Fernand Léger (1881–1955) was a French painter, sculptor, and filmmaker. In his early works, he created a personal form of cubism, which he gradually modified into a more figurative, populist style.

Maurice Merleau-Ponty (1908–61) was a French phenomenological philosopher. The constitution of meaning in human experience was his main interest and he wrote on perception, art, and politics.

Jean-Francois Millet (1814–75) was a French painter and one of the founders of the Barbizon school in rural France. He is noted for his scenes of peasant farmers.

Henry Moore (1898–1986) was an English artist. He is best known for his semi-abstract monumental bronze sculptures.

Laura Mulvey (b. 1941) is a British feminist film theorist. She is best known for her essay and thoughts, "Visual Pleasure and Narrative Cinema," written in 1973 and published in 1975 in the influential British film theory journal *Screen*.

Stephanie O'Donohue is currently Professor of Advertising and Consumer Culture at the University of Edinburgh. She is an interpretive consumer researcher, with a longstanding interest in theories and practices of advertising consumption.

Pablo Picasso (1881–1973) was a Spanish painter, sculptor, printmaker, ceramicist, stage designer, poet, and playwright who spent most of his adult life in France. He is regarded as one of the most influential artists of the twentieth century, and is known for co-founding the Cubism movement.

Griselda Pollock (b. 1949) is a visual theorist and cultural analyst, and scholar of international, postcolonial feminist studies in the visual arts. She is best known for her book *Vision and Difference* (1988) where she provides concrete historical analyses of key moments in the formation of modern culture to reveal the sexual politics at the heart of modernist art.

Jackson Pollock (1912–56) was an American painter and a major figure in the abstract expressionist movement. He was well known for his unique style of drip painting.

Max Raphael (1889–1952) was a German-American art historian. He became the model for Marxist art historians of the later twentieth century.

Rembrandt van Rijn (1606–69) was a prolific Dutch draftsman, painter, and etcher. He is usually regarded as the greatest artist of Holland's Golden Age.

Peter Paul Rubens (1577–1640) was a Flemish painter of religious pictures, mythological scenes, and portraits. He is considered one of the greatest artists of the seventeenth century.

Meyer Shapiro (1904–96) was a Lithuanian-born American art historian. He is best known for forging new art historical methodologies that incorporated an interdisciplinary approach to the study of works of art

Seymour Slive (1920–2014) was an American art historian who served as director of the Harvard Art Museums from 1975 to 1991. He was considered one of the world's leading authorities of seventeenth-century Dutch painting.

Joseph Stalin (1878–1953) was a Soviet revolutionary and political leader. He governed the Soviet Union as dictator from the mid-1920s until his death in 1953.

Vincent van Gogh (1853–90) was a Dutch Post-Impressionist painter. He is among the most famous and influential figures in the history of Western art.

John A. Walker (b. 1938) is a British art critic and historian who has written on modern and contemporary art with an emphasis on mass media.

Raymond Williams (1921–88) was a Welsh academic, novelist, and critic. His writings on politics, culture, the mass media, and literature are a significant contribution to the Marxist critique of culture and the arts.

WORKS CITED

WORKS CITED

ABC Radio. "Exhibit A: John Berger – Changing the Way We See – Part 4." ABC Radio, Accessed July 15, 2017. http://www.abc.net.au/rn/legacy/programs/sunmorn/stories/s1335486.htm.

Barlow, Adrian. *World and Time: Teaching Literature in Context*. Cambridge: Cambridge University Press, 2009.

Bell, Peter. "Realism and Subjectivity in First-Person Shooter Video Games." *Journal of Communication, Culture and Technology* (2003). Accessed July 25, 2017. http://www.gnovisjournal.org/files/Peter-Bell-Realism-and-Subjectivity.pdf.

Benjamin, Walter. "The Work of Art in the Age of Mechanical Reproduction." Translated by Harry Zohn. In *Illuminations: Essays and Reflections*, edited by Hannah Adrendt. London: Cape, 1968.

Berger, John. *Ways of Seeing*. London: Penguin, 2008.

— *Success and Failure of Picasso*. London: Penguin, 1965.

Bil'ak, Peter. "Ways of Seeing – Book Review." *Typotheque*, June 5, 2008. Also in *Back Cover* I (2008). Accessed July 14, 2017. http://www.typotheque.com/articles/ways_of_seeing_book_review.

Christoph, Sara. "Portraits: John Berger on Artists." *The Brooklyn Rail*, February 3, 2016. Accessed June 25, 2017. http://brooklynrail.org/2016/02/art_books/john-berger-on-artists.

Clark, Kenneth. *Civilisation: A Personal View by Kenneth Clark*, directed by Michael Gill. London: BBC, 1969.

— *The Nude*. London: Penguin, 1960.

Davis, Ben. "Ways of Seeing Instagram." *Artnet*, June 24, 2014. Accessed July 4, 2017. https://news.artnet.com/exhibitions/ways-of-seeing-instagram-37635.

— "The Unfinished Business of John Berger." *Artnet*, January 6, 2017. Accessed June 24, 2017. https://news.artnet.com/art-world/the-unfinished-business-of-john-berger-806741.

Dilnot, Clive. "Seven Characteristics of *Ways of Seeing*." *Journal of Visual Culture* 11:2 (August 2012): 148–51.

Dyer, Geoff. "Ways of Witnessing." Interview with John Berger, *Marxism Today* (December 1984), 36–37 (PDF). Accessed June 25, 2017, http://www.unz.org/Pub/MarxismToday-1984dec-00036.

Dyer, Geoff and John Berger. *John Berger/Selected Essays*, edited by Geoff Dyer. London: Bloomsbury, 2001.

Edwards, Mike. *Key Ideas in Media*. Cheltenham, Glos.: Nelson Thornes, 2003.

Fuller, Peter. *Seeing Berger: A Re-evaluation of Ways of Seeing*. London: Writers and Readers, 1980.

— "The Value of Art." *New Society* (1988).

— *Seeing Through Berger*. London: The Claridge Press, 1988.

Gonzalez, Jennifer A. "Calculated Oversight? Resisting Race in *Ways of Seeing*." *Journal of Visual Culture* 11:2 (August 2012): 137–40.

Howells, Richard and Joaquim Negreiros. *Visual Culture*. 2nd ed. Cambridge: Polity Press, 2012.

Hudson, Alan. "John Berger's Ways of Seeing: The Art Critic and the Search for Meaning." *Spiked*, January 25, 2017. Accessed June 21, 2017. http://www.spiked-online.com/newsite/article/john-bergers-ways-of-seeing/19351#.WUqyjyN97-k.

Jay, Martin, "*Ways of Seeing* at Forty." *Journal of Visual Culture* 11: 2 (August 2012): 135–37.

Jones, Amelia, ed. *The Feminism and Visual Culture Reader*. New York: Routledge, 2003.

Kellner, Douglas. "Critical Perspectives on Visual Imagery in Media and Cyberculture." *Journal of Visual Literacy* 22:1 (Spring 2002): 81–90.

Kennedy, Randy. "John Berger, Provocative Art Critic, Dies at 90." *The New York Times*, January 02, 2017. Accessed June 19, 2017. https://www.nytimes.com/2017/01/02/arts/design/john-berger-provocative-art-critic-dies-at-90.html?_r=0.

Kristensen, Juliette. "Making *Ways of Seeing*: A Conversation with Mike Dibb and Richard Hollis." *Journal of Visual Culture* 11: 2 (August 2012): 181–95.

Lambirth, Andrew. "Arts: John Berger: Ways of Seeing, Ways of Biking." *The Independent*, January 17, 1998.

Light, Bob. "John Berger Opened Up New Ways of Seeing." *Socialist Review*, February 2017. Accessed June 20, 2017. http://socialistreview.org.uk/421/john-berger-opened-new-ways-seeing.

Martin McLoone, "Presenters, Artists, and Heroes." *Circa*, 31 (November–December 1986), 10–14.

Maughan, Philip. "'I Think the Dead are With Us': John Berger at 88." *New Statesman*, June 11, 2015. Accessed June 20, 2017. http://www.newstatesman.com/culture/2015/06/i-think-dead-are-us-john-berger-88.

Minto, Robert. "A Smuggling Operation: John Berger's Theory of Art." *Los Angeles Review of Books*, January 2, 2017. Accessed June 25, 2017. https://lareviewofbooks.org/article/a-smuggling-operation-john-bergers-theory-of-art/.

Mulvey, Laura. "Visual Pleasure and Narrative Cinema." *Screen* 16:3 (1975): 6–18.

O'Donohoe, Stephanie. "Living with Ambivalence: Attitudes to Advertising in Postmodern Times." *Marketing Theory* 1:1 (March 2001): 91–108.

O'Hagan, Sean. "A Radical Returns." *The Guardian*, April 03, 2005. Accessed June 19, 2017. https://www.theguardian.com/artanddesign/2005/apr/03/art.art1.

Pollock, Griselda. "Muscular Defences." *Journal of Visual Culture* 11: 2 (August 2012): 127–31.

Rai, Pratibha. "Review: 'Ways of Seeing'." *The Oxford Culture Review*, April 04, 2017. Accessed July 03, 2017. https://theoxfordculturereview.com/2017/04/04/review-ways-of-seeing/.

Richardson, John Adkins, "Ways of Seeing by John Berger." *The Journal of Aesthetic Education*, 8:4 (October 1974): 111–13.

— "Seeing Berger: A Revaluation of 'Ways of Seeing' by Peter Fuller." *Leonardo*, 16:1, (Winter 1983): 66.

Rogers, Heather. "Still Seeing: Berger's Critique of High Art Turns 30." In *The Brooklyn Rail: Critical Perspectives on Arts, Politics and Culture* (Autumn 2002). Accessed July 15, 2017. http://brooklynrail.org/2002/10/books/still-seeing-bergers-critique-of-high-ar.

Steven, Peter. "The Ways of Seeing – against Kenneth Clark, for John Berger." *Jump Cut: A Review of Contemporary Media* 20 (May 1979): 7–8.

Sturken, Marita. "Ways of Seeing, Practices of Looking." *Journal of Visual Culture* 11:2 (August 2012): 151–53.

Tepper, Anderson. "At Work: John Berger on *Bento's Sketchbook*." *The Paris Review* (November 22, 2011). Accessed June 11, 2017. https://www.theparisreview.org/blog/2011/11/22/john-berger-on-%E2%80%98bento%E2%80%99s-sketchbook%E2%80%99/.

The Art Newspaper. "John Berger, the Author of Ways of Seeing, has died aged 90," Obituary, *The Art Newspaper*, January 3, 2017. Accessed July 23, 2017. http://theartnewspaper.com/news/obituary/john-berger-the-author-of-ways-of-seeing-has-died-aged-90.

Walker, John. *Arts TV: A History of Arts Television in Britain*. London: John Libbey and Company Ltd, 1993.

THE MACAT LIBRARY
BY DISCIPLINE

The Macat Library By Discipline

AFRICANA STUDIES

Chinua Achebe's *An Image of Africa: Racism in Conrad's Heart of Darkness*
W. E. B. Du Bois's *The Souls of Black Folk*
Zora Neale Huston's *Characteristics of Negro Expression*
Martin Luther King Jr's *Why We Can't Wait*
Toni Morrison's *Playing in the Dark: Whiteness in the American Literary Imagination*

ANTHROPOLOGY

Arjun Appadurai's *Modernity at Large: Cultural Dimensions of Globalisation*
Philippe Ariès's *Centuries of Childhood*
Franz Boas's *Race, Language and Culture*
Kim Chan & Renée Mauborgne's *Blue Ocean Strategy*
Jared Diamond's *Guns, Germs & Steel: the Fate of Human Societies*
Jared Diamond's *Collapse: How Societies Choose to Fail or Survive*
E. E. Evans-Pritchard's *Witchcraft, Oracles and Magic Among the Azande*
James Ferguson's *The Anti-Politics Machine*
Clifford Geertz's *The Interpretation of Cultures*
David Graeber's *Debt: the First 5000 Years*
Karen Ho's *Liquidated: An Ethnography of Wall Street*
Geert Hofstede's *Culture's Consequences: Comparing Values, Behaviors, Institutes and Organizations across Nations*
Claude Lévi-Strauss's *Structural Anthropology*
Jay Macleod's *Ain't No Makin' It: Aspirations and Attainment in a Low-Income Neighborhood*
Saba Mahmood's *The Politics of Piety: The Islamic Revival and the Feminist Subject*
Marcel Mauss's *The Gift*

BUSINESS

Jean Lave & Etienne Wenger's *Situated Learning*
Theodore Levitt's *Marketing Myopia*
Burton G. Malkiel's *A Random Walk Down Wall Street*
Douglas McGregor's *The Human Side of Enterprise*
Michael Porter's *Competitive Strategy: Creating and Sustaining Superior Performance*
John Kotter's *Leading Change*
C. K. Prahalad & Gary Hamel's *The Core Competence of the Corporation*

CRIMINOLOGY

Michelle Alexander's *The New Jim Crow: Mass Incarceration in the Age of Colorblindness*
Michael R. Gottfredson & Travis Hirschi's *A General Theory of Crime*
Richard Herrnstein & Charles A. Murray's *The Bell Curve: Intelligence and Class Structure in American Life*
Elizabeth Loftus's *Eyewitness Testimony*
Jay Macleod's *Ain't No Makin' It: Aspirations and Attainment in a Low-Income Neighborhood*
Philip Zimbardo's *The Lucifer Effect*

ECONOMICS

Janet Abu-Lughod's *Before European Hegemony*
Ha-Joon Chang's *Kicking Away the Ladder*
David Brion Davis's *The Problem of Slavery in the Age of Revolution*
Milton Friedman's *The Role of Monetary Policy*
Milton Friedman's *Capitalism and Freedom*
David Graeber's *Debt: the First 5000 Years*
Friedrich Hayek's *The Road to Serfdom*
Karen Ho's *Liquidated: An Ethnography of Wall Street*

John Maynard Keynes's *The General Theory of Employment, Interest and Money*
Charles P. Kindleberger's *Manias, Panics and Crashes*
Robert Lucas's *Why Doesn't Capital Flow from Rich to Poor Countries?*
Burton G. Malkiel's *A Random Walk Down Wall Street*
Thomas Robert Malthus's *An Essay on the Principle of Population*
Karl Marx's *Capital*
Thomas Piketty's *Capital in the Twenty-First Century*
Amartya Sen's *Development as Freedom*
Adam Smith's *The Wealth of Nations*
Nassim Nicholas Taleb's *The Black Swan: The Impact of the Highly Improbable*
Amos Tversky's & Daniel Kahneman's *Judgment under Uncertainty: Heuristics and Biases*
Mahbub Ul Haq's *Reflections on Human Development*
Max Weber's *The Protestant Ethic and the Spirit of Capitalism*

FEMINISM AND GENDER STUDIES

Judith Butler's *Gender Trouble*
Simone De Beauvoir's *The Second Sex*
Michel Foucault's *History of Sexuality*
Betty Friedan's *The Feminine Mystique*
Saba Mahmood's *The Politics of Piety: The Islamic Revival and the Feminist Subject*
Joan Wallach Scott's *Gender and the Politics of History*
Mary Wollstonecraft's *A Vindication of the Rights of Woman*
Virginia Woolf's *A Room of One's Own*

GEOGRAPHY

The Brundtland Report's *Our Common Future*
Rachel Carson's *Silent Spring*
Charles Darwin's *On the Origin of Species*
James Ferguson's *The Anti-Politics Machine*
Jane Jacobs's *The Death and Life of Great American Cities*
James Lovelock's *Gaia: A New Look at Life on Earth*
Amartya Sen's *Development as Freedom*
Mathis Wackernagel & William Rees's *Our Ecological Footprint*

HISTORY

Janet Abu-Lughod's *Before European Hegemony*
Benedict Anderson's *Imagined Communities*
Bernard Bailyn's *The Ideological Origins of the American Revolution*
Hanna Batatu's *The Old Social Classes And The Revolutionary Movements Of Iraq*
Christopher Browning's *Ordinary Men: Reserve Police Batallion 101 and the Final Solution in Poland*
Edmund Burke's *Reflections on the Revolution in France*
William Cronon's *Nature's Metropolis: Chicago And The Great West*
Alfred W. Crosby's *The Columbian Exchange*
Hamid Dabashi's *Iran: A People Interrupted*
David Brion Davis's *The Problem of Slavery in the Age of Revolution*
Nathalie Zemon Davis's *The Return of Martin Guerre*
Jared Diamond's *Guns, Germs & Steel: the Fate of Human Societies*
Frank Dikotter's *Mao's Great Famine*
John W Dower's *War Without Mercy: Race And Power In The Pacific War*
W. E. B. Du Bois's *The Souls of Black Folk*
Richard J. Evans's *In Defence of History*
Lucien Febvre's *The Problem of Unbelief in the 16th Century*
Sheila Fitzpatrick's *Everyday Stalinism*

The Macat Library By Discipline

Eric Foner's *Reconstruction: America's Unfinished Revolution, 1863-1877*
Michel Foucault's *Discipline and Punish*
Michel Foucault's *History of Sexuality*
Francis Fukuyama's *The End of History and the Last Man*
John Lewis Gaddis's *We Now Know: Rethinking Cold War History*
Ernest Gellner's *Nations and Nationalism*
Eugene Genovese's *Roll, Jordan, Roll: The World the Slaves Made*
Carlo Ginzburg's *The Night Battles*
Daniel Goldhagen's *Hitler's Willing Executioners*
Jack Goldstone's *Revolution and Rebellion in the Early Modern World*
Antonio Gramsci's *The Prison Notebooks*
Alexander Hamilton, John Jay & James Madison's *The Federalist Papers*
Christopher Hill's *The World Turned Upside Down*
Carole Hillenbrand's *The Crusades: Islamic Perspectives*
Thomas Hobbes's *Leviathan*
Eric Hobsbawm's *The Age Of Revolution*
John A. Hobson's *Imperialism: A Study*
Albert Hourani's *History of the Arab Peoples*
Samuel P. Huntington's *The Clash of Civilizations and the Remaking of World Order*
C. L. R. James's *The Black Jacobins*
Tony Judt's *Postwar: A History of Europe Since 1945*
Ernst Kantorowicz's *The King's Two Bodies: A Study in Medieval Political Theology*
Paul Kennedy's *The Rise and Fall of the Great Powers*
Ian Kershaw's *The "Hitler Myth": Image and Reality in the Third Reich*
John Maynard Keynes's *The General Theory of Employment, Interest and Money*
Charles P. Kindleberger's *Manias, Panics and Crashes*
Martin Luther King Jr's *Why We Can't Wait*
Henry Kissinger's *World Order: Reflections on the Character of Nations and the Course of History*
Thomas Kuhn's *The Structure of Scientific Revolutions*
Georges Lefebvre's *The Coming of the French Revolution*
John Locke's *Two Treatises of Government*
Niccolò Machiavelli's *The Prince*
Thomas Robert Malthus's *An Essay on the Principle of Population*
Mahmood Mamdani's *Citizen and Subject: Contemporary Africa And The Legacy Of Late Colonialism*
Karl Marx's *Capital*
Stanley Milgram's *Obedience to Authority*
John Stuart Mill's *On Liberty*
Thomas Paine's *Common Sense*
Thomas Paine's *Rights of Man*
Geoffrey Parker's *Global Crisis: War, Climate Change and Catastrophe in the Seventeenth Century*
Jonathan Riley-Smith's *The First Crusade and the Idea of Crusading*
Jean-Jacques Rousseau's *The Social Contract*
Joan Wallach Scott's *Gender and the Politics of History*
Theda Skocpol's *States and Social Revolutions*
Adam Smith's *The Wealth of Nations*
Timothy Snyder's *Bloodlands: Europe Between Hitler and Stalin*
Sun Tzu's *The Art of War*
Keith Thomas's *Religion and the Decline of Magic*
Thucydides's *The History of the Peloponnesian War*
Frederick Jackson Turner's *The Significance of the Frontier in American History*
Odd Arne Westad's *The Global Cold War: Third World Interventions And The Making Of Our Times*

LITERATURE

Chinua Achebe's *An Image of Africa: Racism in Conrad's Heart of Darkness*
Roland Barthes's *Mythologies*
Homi K. Bhabha's *The Location of Culture*
Judith Butler's *Gender Trouble*
Simone De Beauvoir's *The Second Sex*
Ferdinand De Saussure's *Course in General Linguistics*
T. S. Eliot's *The Sacred Wood: Essays on Poetry and Criticism*
Zora Neale Huston's *Characteristics of Negro Expression*
Toni Morrison's *Playing in the Dark: Whiteness in the American Literary Imagination*
Edward Said's *Orientalism*
Gayatri Chakravorty Spivak's *Can the Subaltern Speak?*
Mary Wollstonecraft's *A Vindication of the Rights of Women*
Virginia Woolf's *A Room of One's Own*

PHILOSOPHY

Elizabeth Anscombe's *Modern Moral Philosophy*
Hannah Arendt's *The Human Condition*
Aristotle's *Metaphysics*
Aristotle's *Nicomachean Ethics*
Edmund Gettier's *Is Justified True Belief Knowledge?*
Georg Wilhelm Friedrich Hegel's *Phenomenology of Spirit*
David Hume's *Dialogues Concerning Natural Religion*
David Hume's *The Enquiry for Human Understanding*
Immanuel Kant's *Religion within the Boundaries of Mere Reason*
Immanuel Kant's *Critique of Pure Reason*
Søren Kierkegaard's *The Sickness Unto Death*
Søren Kierkegaard's *Fear and Trembling*
C. S. Lewis's *The Abolition of Man*
Alasdair MacIntyre's *After Virtue*
Marcus Aurelius's *Meditations*
Friedrich Nietzsche's *On the Genealogy of Morality*
Friedrich Nietzsche's *Beyond Good and Evil*
Plato's *Republic*
Plato's *Symposium*
Jean-Jacques Rousseau's *The Social Contract*
Gilbert Ryle's *The Concept of Mind*
Baruch Spinoza's *Ethics*
Sun Tzu's *The Art of War*
Ludwig Wittgenstein's *Philosophical Investigations*

POLITICS

Benedict Anderson's *Imagined Communities*
Aristotle's *Politics*
Bernard Bailyn's *The Ideological Origins of the American Revolution*
Edmund Burke's *Reflections on the Revolution in France*
John C. Calhoun's *A Disquisition on Government*
Ha-Joon Chang's *Kicking Away the Ladder*
Hamid Dabashi's *Iran: A People Interrupted*
Hamid Dabashi's *Theology of Discontent: The Ideological Foundation of the Islamic Revolution in Iran*
Robert Dahl's *Democracy and its Critics*
Robert Dahl's *Who Governs?*
David Brion Davis's *The Problem of Slavery in the Age of Revolution*

The Macat Library By Discipline

Alexis De Tocqueville's *Democracy in America*
James Ferguson's *The Anti-Politics Machine*
Frank Dikotter's *Mao's Great Famine*
Sheila Fitzpatrick's *Everyday Stalinism*
Eric Foner's *Reconstruction: America's Unfinished Revolution, 1863-1877*
Milton Friedman's *Capitalism and Freedom*
Francis Fukuyama's *The End of History and the Last Man*
John Lewis Gaddis's *We Now Know: Rethinking Cold War History*
Ernest Gellner's *Nations and Nationalism*
David Graeber's *Debt: the First 5000 Years*
Antonio Gramsci's *The Prison Notebooks*
Alexander Hamilton, John Jay & James Madison's *The Federalist Papers*
Friedrich Hayek's *The Road to Serfdom*
Christopher Hill's *The World Turned Upside Down*
Thomas Hobbes's *Leviathan*
John A. Hobson's *Imperialism: A Study*
Samuel P. Huntington's *The Clash of Civilizations and the Remaking of World Order*
Tony Judt's *Postwar: A History of Europe Since 1945*
David C. Kang's *China Rising: Peace, Power and Order in East Asia*
Paul Kennedy's *The Rise and Fall of Great Powers*
Robert Keohane's *After Hegemony*
Martin Luther King Jr.'s *Why We Can't Wait*
Henry Kissinger's *World Order: Reflections on the Character of Nations and the Course of History*
John Locke's *Two Treatises of Government*
Niccolò Machiavelli's *The Prince*
Thomas Robert Malthus's *An Essay on the Principle of Population*
Mahmood Mamdani's *Citizen and Subject: Contemporary Africa And The Legacy Of Late Colonialism*
Karl Marx's *Capital*
John Stuart Mill's *On Liberty*
John Stuart Mill's *Utilitarianism*
Hans Morgenthau's *Politics Among Nations*
Thomas Paine's *Common Sense*
Thomas Paine's *Rights of Man*
Thomas Piketty's *Capital in the Twenty-First Century*
Robert D. Putman's *Bowling Alone*
John Rawls's *Theory of Justice*
Jean-Jacques Rousseau's *The Social Contract*
Theda Skocpol's *States and Social Revolutions*
Adam Smith's *The Wealth of Nations*
Sun Tzu's *The Art of War*
Henry David Thoreau's *Civil Disobedience*
Thucydides's *The History of the Peloponnesian War*
Kenneth Waltz's *Theory of International Politics*
Max Weber's *Politics as a Vocation*
Odd Arne Westad's *The Global Cold War: Third World Interventions And The Making Of Our Times*

POSTCOLONIAL STUDIES

Roland Barthes's *Mythologies*
Frantz Fanon's *Black Skin, White Masks*
Homi K. Bhabha's *The Location of Culture*
Gustavo Gutiérrez's *A Theology of Liberation*
Edward Said's *Orientalism*
Gayatri Chakravorty Spivak's *Can the Subaltern Speak?*

PSYCHOLOGY

Gordon Allport's *The Nature of Prejudice*
Alan Baddeley & Graham Hitch's *Aggression: A Social Learning Analysis*
Albert Bandura's *Aggression: A Social Learning Analysis*
Leon Festinger's *A Theory of Cognitive Dissonance*
Sigmund Freud's *The Interpretation of Dreams*
Betty Friedan's *The Feminine Mystique*
Michael R. Gottfredson & Travis Hirschi's *A General Theory of Crime*
Eric Hoffer's *The True Believer: Thoughts on the Nature of Mass Movements*
William James's *Principles of Psychology*
Elizabeth Loftus's *Eyewitness Testimony*
A. H. Maslow's *A Theory of Human Motivation*
Stanley Milgram's *Obedience to Authority*
Steven Pinker's *The Better Angels of Our Nature*
Oliver Sacks's *The Man Who Mistook His Wife For a Hat*
Richard Thaler & Cass Sunstein's *Nudge: Improving Decisions About Health, Wealth and Happiness*
Amos Tversky's *Judgment under Uncertainty: Heuristics and Biases*
Philip Zimbardo's *The Lucifer Effect*

SCIENCE

Rachel Carson's *Silent Spring*
William Cronon's *Nature's Metropolis: Chicago And The Great West*
Alfred W. Crosby's *The Columbian Exchange*
Charles Darwin's *On the Origin of Species*
Richard Dawkin's *The Selfish Gene*
Thomas Kuhn's *The Structure of Scientific Revolutions*
Geoffrey Parker's *Global Crisis: War, Climate Change and Catastrophe in the Seventeenth Century*
Mathis Wackernagel & William Rees's *Our Ecological Footprint*

SOCIOLOGY

Michelle Alexander's *The New Jim Crow: Mass Incarceration in the Age of Colorblindness*
Gordon Allport's *The Nature of Prejudice*
Albert Bandura's *Aggression: A Social Learning Analysis*
Hanna Batatu's *The Old Social Classes And The Revolutionary Movements Of Iraq*
Ha-Joon Chang's *Kicking Away the Ladder*
W. E. B. Du Bois's *The Souls of Black Folk*
Émile Durkheim's *On Suicide*
Frantz Fanon's *Black Skin, White Masks*
Frantz Fanon's *The Wretched of the Earth*
Eric Foner's *Reconstruction: America's Unfinished Revolution, 1863-1877*
Eugene Genovese's *Roll, Jordan, Roll: The World the Slaves Made*
Jack Goldstone's *Revolution and Rebellion in the Early Modern World*
Antonio Gramsci's *The Prison Notebooks*
Richard Herrnstein & Charles A Murray's *The Bell Curve: Intelligence and Class Structure in American Life*
Eric Hoffer's *The True Believer: Thoughts on the Nature of Mass Movements*
Jane Jacobs's *The Death and Life of Great American Cities*
Robert Lucas's *Why Doesn't Capital Flow from Rich to Poor Countries?*
Jay Macleod's *Ain't No Makin' It: Aspirations and Attainment in a Low Income Neighborhood*
Elaine May's *Homeward Bound: American Families in the Cold War Era*
Douglas McGregor's *The Human Side of Enterprise*
C. Wright Mills's *The Sociological Imagination*

The Macat Library By Discipline

Thomas Piketty's *Capital in the Twenty-First Century*
Robert D. Putman's *Bowling Alone*
David Riesman's *The Lonely Crowd: A Study of the Changing American Character*
Edward Said's *Orientalism*
Joan Wallach Scott's *Gender and the Politics of History*
Theda Skocpol's *States and Social Revolutions*
Max Weber's *The Protestant Ethic and the Spirit of Capitalism*

THEOLOGY

Augustine's *Confessions*
Benedict's *Rule of St Benedict*
Gustavo Gutiérrez's *A Theology of Liberation*
Carole Hillenbrand's *The Crusades: Islamic Perspectives*
David Hume's *Dialogues Concerning Natural Religion*
Immanuel Kant's *Religion within the Boundaries of Mere Reason*
Ernst Kantorowicz's *The King's Two Bodies: A Study in Medieval Political Theology*
Søren Kierkegaard's *The Sickness Unto Death*
C. S. Lewis's *The Abolition of Man*
Saba Mahmood's *The Politics of Piety: The Islamic Revival and the Feminist Subject*
Baruch Spinoza's *Ethics*
Keith Thomas's *Religion and the Decline of Magic*

COMING SOON

Chris Argyris's *The Individual and the Organisation*
Seyla Benhabib's *The Rights of Others*
Walter Benjamin's *The Work Of Art in the Age of Mechanical Reproduction*
John Berger's *Ways of Seeing*
Pierre Bourdieu's *Outline of a Theory of Practice*
Mary Douglas's *Purity and Danger*
Roland Dworkin's *Taking Rights Seriously*
James G. March's *Exploration and Exploitation in Organisational Learning*
Ikujiro Nonaka's *A Dynamic Theory of Organizational Knowledge Creation*
Griselda Pollock's *Vision and Difference*
Amartya Sen's *Inequality Re-Examined*
Susan Sontag's *On Photography*
Yasser Tabbaa's *The Transformation of Islamic Art*
Ludwig von Mises's *Theory of Money and Credit*

Macat Disciplines

Access the greatest ideas and thinkers across entire disciplines, including

Postcolonial Studies

Roland Barthes's *Mythologies*
Frantz Fanon's *Black Skin, White Masks*
Homi K. Bhabha's *The Location of Culture*
Gustavo Gutiérrez's *A Theology of Liberation*
Edward Said's *Orientalism*
Gayatri Chakravorty Spivak's *Can the Subaltern Speak?*

Macat Disciplines

Access the greatest ideas and thinkers across entire disciplines, including

AFRICANA STUDIES

Chinua Achebe's *An Image of Africa: Racism in Conrad's Heart of Darkness*

W. E. B. Du Bois's *The Souls of Black Folk*

Zora Neale Hurston's *Characteristics of Negro Expression*

Martin Luther King Jr.'s *Why We Can't Wait*

Toni Morrison's *Playing in the Dark: Whiteness in the American Literary Imagination*

Macat analyses are available from all good bookshops and libraries.

Access hundreds of analyses through one, multimedia tool.
Join free for one month **library.macat.com**

Macat Disciplines

Access the greatest ideas and thinkers across entire disciplines, including

FEMINISM, GENDER AND QUEER STUDIES

Simone De Beauvoir's
The Second Sex

Michel Foucault's
History of Sexuality

Betty Friedan's
The Feminine Mystique

Saba Mahmood's
*The Politics of Piety:
The Islamic Revival and
the Feminist Subject*

Joan Wallach Scott's
*Gender and the
Politics of History*

Mary Wollstonecraft's
*A Vindication of the
Rights of Woman*

Virginia Woolf's
A Room of One's Own

Judith Butler's
Gender Trouble

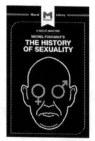

Macat analyses are available from all good bookshops and libraries.

Access hundreds of analyses through one, multimedia tool.
Join free for one month **library.macat.com**

Macat Disciplines

Access the greatest ideas and thinkers across entire disciplines, including

CRIMINOLOGY

Michelle Alexander's
*The New Jim Crow:
Mass Incarceration in the
Age of Colorblindness*

**Michael R. Gottfredson
& Travis Hirschi's**
A General Theory of Crime

Elizabeth Loftus's
Eyewitness Testimony

**Richard Herrnstein
& Charles A. Murray's**
*The Bell Curve: Intelligence and
Class Structure in American Life*

Jay Macleod's
*Ain't No Makin' It:
Aspirations and Attainment in a
Low-Income Neighborhood*

Philip Zimbardo's
The Lucifer Effect

Macat analyses are available from all good bookshops and libraries.

Access hundreds of analyses through one, multimedia tool.

Join free for one month **library.macat.com**

Macat Disciplines

Access the greatest ideas and thinkers across entire disciplines, including

INEQUALITY

Ha-Joon Chang's, *Kicking Away the Ladder*
David Graeber's, *Debt: The First 5000 Years*
Robert E. Lucas's, *Why Doesn't Capital Flow from Rich To Poor Countries?*
Thomas Piketty's, *Capital in the Twenty-First Century*
Amartya Sen's, *Inequality Re-Examined*
Mahbub Ul Haq's, *Reflections on Human Development*

Macat analyses are available from all good bookshops and libraries.

Access hundreds of analyses through one, multimedia tool.

Join free for one month **library.macat.com**

Macat Disciplines

Access the greatest ideas and thinkers across entire disciplines, including

GLOBALIZATION

Arjun Appadurai's, *Modernity at Large: Cultural Dimensions of Globalisation*

James Ferguson's, *The Anti-Politics Machine*

Geert Hofstede's, *Culture's Consequences*

Amartya Sen's, *Development as Freedom*

Macat Disciplines

Access the greatest ideas and thinkers across entire disciplines, including

MAN AND THE ENVIRONMENT

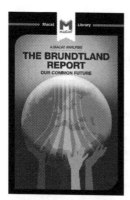

The Brundtland Report's, *Our Common Future*
Rachel Carson's, *Silent Spring*
James Lovelock's, *Gaia: A New Look at Life on Earth*
Mathis Wackernagel & William Rees's, *Our Ecological Footprint*

Macat analyses are available from all good bookshops and libraries.

Access hundreds of analyses through one, multimedia tool.
Join free for one month **library.macat.com**

Macat Disciplines

Access the greatest ideas and thinkers across entire disciplines, including

THE FUTURE OF DEMOCRACY

Robert A. Dahl's, *Democracy and Its Critics*
Robert A. Dahl's, *Who Governs?*
Alexis De Toqueville's, *Democracy in America*
Niccolò Machiavelli's, *The Prince*
John Stuart Mill's, *On Liberty*
Robert D. Putnam's, *Bowling Alone*
Jean-Jacques Rousseau's, *The Social Contract*
Henry David Thoreau's, *Civil Disobedience*

Macat analyses are available from all good bookshops and libraries.

Access hundreds of analyses through one, multimedia tool.
Join free for one month **library.macat.com**

Printed in the United States
by Baker & Taylor Publisher Services